RENZO CHIARELLI

VERONA

History and Masterpieces

255 COLOR PHOTOGRAPHS

CITY MAP

BONECHI EDIZIONI "IL TURISMO"

Concessionary Agent for Verona:
Randazzo G. S.n.c. di Randazzo E. & R.
Via Emilei, 22 - 37121 VERONA
Tel. +39-045 800.40.40
Fax +39-045 803.60.63

Reprint 2003

Copyright 2002 by Bonechi Edizioni "Il Turismo" S.r.l.
Via dei Rustici, 5 - 50122 FIRENZE
Tel. +39-055 239.82.24
Fax +39-055 21.63.66
E-mail: bbonechi@dada.it
        info@bonechionline.com
http: //www.bonechionline.com
Printed in Italy
All rights reserved

Publishing Manager: Barbara Bonechi
Coordination and revision of texts and iconographical research: Lorena Lazzari
Graphic design and layout: Paola Rufino
Photo credits: Archives of Bonechi Edizioni "Il Turismo", photographer
Nicola Grifoni (Florence).
Photo on page 45, permission kindly granted by the Italian Ministry of
Cultural Assets and Environment, "Soprintendenza SBAS del Veneto".
Photos on pages 29, 30, 38: Di Giovine Photografica (Verona)
Photolithography: Fotolito Immagine, Florence
Printing: STIAV S.r.l., Florence

ISBN 88-7204-518-5

VERONA "GATEWAY TO ITALY"

Verona, *Urbs Nobilissima*, is one of the most beautiful and ancient of all Italian cities – one which is justly famous and beloved both in Italy, and indeed, throughout the whole world. Today Verona has about 270,000 inhabitants, and in the whole district of Veneto it is second only to Venice in wealth and importance.

Its climate and accessibility are ideal, and Verona is a vital rail and road junction on the main route connecting Italy to Central Europe. It is a flourishing industrial, commercial and agricultural centre of international importance and is the site of the annual *International Agricultural Show* and the *International Exhibi-tion of Agricultural Machinery* – just two of the city's large exhibitions which attract visitors from all over Europe. The city is important in other fields as well – it is the home of the Mondadori publishing house, famous the world over. While on the subject of commerce, mention must be made of its wines, fruit, and of its marble, all of which are exported to many countries. Because of its fortunate geographical position and its importance as a European city, Verona has been described as the *Gateway to Italy*. To travellers approaching from the North there is another sense in which Verona can be thought of as the *Gateway to Italy*. It is the first city which clearly possesses the appearance, harmony, character, the tradition and beauty of Italy, giving, as it were, a foretaste of the fundamental characteristics of the country as a whole. Verona's undeniable beauty has been celebrated by many foreign visitors who, from the earliest times have continued to pay tribute to the town in poetry and prose. Its beauty is essentially two-fold. Firstly, it is rich in natural beauty with its river, its hills, the nearby Lake Garda, and its background of

▼ *Night view of Verona*

"THERE IS NO WORLD WITHOVT VERONA WALLS,
BVT PVRGATORY, TORTVRE, HELL ITSELF,
HENCE BANISHED IS BANISH'D FROM THE WORLD,
AND WORLD'S EXILE IS DEATH; . . . ."

"NON ESISTE MONDO FVOR DALLE MVRA DI VERONA;
MA SOLO PVRGATORIO, TORTVRA, INFERNO.
CHI E BANDITO DI QVI, E BANDITO DAL MONDO
E L'ESILIO DAL MONDO E MORTE; . . . ."

(SHAKESPEARE, "ROMEO AND JVLIET", ATTO III, SCENA III)

mountains. Secondly, there is the great architectural beauty of the city itself with its buildings and monuments. Verona is also an important cultural centre. It is a university city, with faculties of Economics, Languages, Education and Medicine, and a city rich in museums and distinguished libraries. But it is not just as an academic city that Verona has found fame, it has also become one of the major tourist centres of Italy. This is not surprising since the city as a whole is outstanding in what it has to offer the tourist. The people of Verona are friendly and welcoming, and a great deal of trouble is taken to make sure that visitors really enjoy their stay. There are, for example, theatrical performances staged during the warmer months, which include *operas in the Roman Arena* and *Shakespeare's plays* staged in the Roman Theatre. There are Concert and Drama Societies and a highly renowned Academy of Music (Conservatorio di Musica). Finally we come to the one tourist attraction which makes Verona absolutely unique – its reputation thanks to Shakespeare and his play, as being the town of *Romeo and Juliet*.

This, then, is the city that we have set out briefly to describe, with its traditions, its fine buildings, its distinguished monuments, so that visitors may remember her by and, perhaps, may want to come back some day.

▼ *View of the Arena*

The origins of Verona are lost in the mists of time; it is not even known how the city came by its name. All that can be said with certainty is that it was in prehistoric times that human beings first settled in the place where the city was later to rise. The date of the first Roman occupation is not known for sure, but by the 1st century B.C. Verona was already an important Roman settlement and the ancient centre of the town preserves the outlines of the original Roman nucleus which was known as *Colonia Augusta Verona*. Most of the important Roman remains in the town date from the 1st century B.C. The town centre, like all towns founded on Roman military camps is divided by the "cardus" and the "decumanus" – at right angles to each other – into four "quarters". In the number and quality of its Roman remains – the Amphitheatre, the Theatre, the arches, gates, and bridges etc. – Verona is second only to Rome itself. From very early days Verona's geographical position was a vital factor in the city's importance. Three

▲ *Detail of the Porta Borsari*

of the most important Roman roads started from there – the Augusta, the Gallica, and the Postumia. The city's importance as a strategic centre, which was to last nearly a thousand years, became evident as early as the Late Empire. During this period, several decisive battles were fought in the neighbourhood of Verona, such as the battles of Claudius against the Germans in 268 A.D., Constantine against Maxentius in 312 A.D., and Stilicho against Alaric in 402 A.D. Even as early as the Roman period, Verona had already become a cultural centre and produced one of the greatest Latin poets: Q. Valerius Catullus.

In the Middle Ages, Verona was again the scene of important events. Theodoric stayed there, as did Alboin, the Longobard, who was murdered in Verona by his wife Rosamund. Later, Pepin, the son of Charlemagne, visited Verona as did Berengarius, the latter dying there in 924 in tragic circumstances.

Emperor Otto I of Germany came to the city to rescue Adelaide of Burgundy, who was held prisoner in the area. Despite invasions and wars, however, Verona still remained loyal to its cultural heritage. The city was fortunate in coming under the influence of two noble churchmen – the great Bishop St. Zeno during the 4th century and the kindly Archdeacon Pacifico

◄ *Remnants of the ancient Roman road at the foot of the Arch of the Gavii*

in the 9th century. Under the latter, there flourished one of the most famous Academies of the period, the *Schola Sacerdotum*. The city developed its own distinctive style of art, and this, combined with the influence of the Carolingian and Ottonian style, enriched the city with Early Christian basilicas and Pre-Romanesque churches. At about this time also, the *Palace of Theodoric* was beginning to take shape on the banks of the River Adige.

During the troubled times of the early 12th century, the Commune of Verona was formed. The city became deeply involved in the bitter wars which swept through the whole country. The greatest of these involved the conflicts between the Papacy and the Empire. In addition there were many purely local wars between neighbouring cities. But in spite of these conflicts, Verona flourished, not only in trade, but also in the arts, and as a political centre. In 1164, under this first Council, the *Alliance of Verona* came into being. This united all the mainland cities of the Veneto against Barbarossa and was to lead to the subsequent League of Lombardy. In 1226, Verona became a possession of the tyrannical Ezzelino da Romano. Then in 1262, Leonardino della Scala nicknamed Mastino, was voted lord of the city, and thus began the rule of the great Scala (or Scaliger) family. Mastino was succeeded by Alberto, who died in 1301, and after him came his sons Bartolomeo, Alboino and Can Francesco. In 1308, Can Francesco became lord of the city, under the name Cangrande I. During his rule, the dominance of the Scala family reached its most glorious height, with the city extending its influence over nearly all mainland Veneto. Cangrande, using his powers as the ruler of Verona, made the city into an antipapal stronghold. Its court became a cultural refuge and artists and writers flocked there in great number. Dante himself, who had previously been the guest of Cangrande's brother Bartolomeo, dedicated the third section of the Divine Comedy to his friend and patron, Cangrande. The death of Cangrande in 1329 marked the beginning of Verona's decline, despite the influence of a succession of distinguished rulers. One of them was Mastino II, under whose rule the sway of the Scala family was extended to include Brescia, Parma and Lucca. There was also Cangrande II, who built Castelvecchio and the superb bridge next to it, and then came the ferocious Cansignorio.

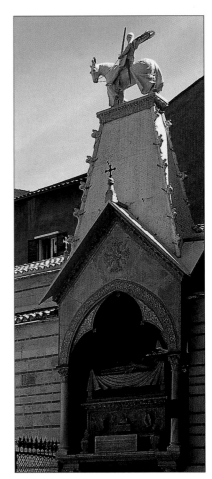

▲ *Tomb of Cangrande I della Scala*

The other great Italian ruling families, particularly those of Venice and Florence, often formed alliances against the Scalas, as did the Papacy itself. The rule of the Scala family finally came to an end with the flight of Antonio della Scala in 1387, after which the city fell into the hands of Gian Galeazzo Visconti. In 1404, Verona was conquered by the Carraresi, a powerful family from Padua; in 1405 it became part of the Venetian state. Venice retained its control over the city for nearly four hundred years, except for a brief period from 1509 to 1517, when Maximilian of Austria conquered it. Although the Venetian influence gave Verona a long period of relative peace and prosperity, any suggestion of independence or desire for autonomy was firmly suppressed. As a result, the spirit and atmosphere of the city suffered severely. Verona's greatest artistic and cultural

A
DANTE
LO PRIMO SVO RIFVGIO
NELLE FESTE NEI VOTI
CONCORDE
OGNI TERRA ITALIANA

XIV MAGGIO MDCCCLXV
DC SVO NATALIZIO

◀ *Monument to Dante, Piazza dei Signori*

▲ The façade of San Zeno Maggiore,
a typical example of Romanesque architecture

and stonemasons of the 13th and 14th centuries. These men were primarily inspired by the great masters Nicolò and Guglielmo, but they were also open to other influences ranging from Venetian and Byzantine to the Wiligelmic, Carolingian and Ottonian. The finest products of this group of sculptors are the magnificent doors of the Cathedral and San Zeno, and the 14th century funeral monument to the Scala family, towering over which stands the impressive equestrian statue of Cangrande della Scala. The earliest frescoes of note are those in the Chapel of San Nazaro painted in the 10th century, and even these early attempts are outstanding. Later frescoes, such as the early 14th century ones, clearly show the influence of Giotto and examples of these are to be found in San Fermo. There was, however, no distinct "school" as such,

▼ View of Sant'Anastasia,
outstanding example of Gothic architecture

achievements came during the three centuries when the Commune and the Scala family were in power. It was in this period that Verona's splendid townscape, which survives to this day, was mostly built. Although Verona did not lack poets and writers, such as Giacomino da Verona and Gidino da Sommacampagna, the city's greatest artistic achievements were in the field of sculpture and architecture.

There are some outstanding examples of the Romanesque style in Verona such as the churches of the Santissima Trinità, Santo Stefano, San Lorenzo, San Zeno, San Giovanni in Valle, the Lower Church of San Fermo, etc. The Gothic style is exemplified by, among the churches, Sant'Anastasia, the greater part of the Cathedral, San Fermo, and among non-religious buildings by the Castelvecchio and the tombs of the Scala family. There is a great deal of very impressive sculpture in Verona, by unknown or little known craftsmen

until the middle of the 14th century when Turone actually founded the Veronese school. He was followed by Altichiero, the famous artist, who worked both in Padua and Verona. As a result of Verona's unique position as an intermediary amongst widely diverse cultures, the city became one of the main centres of the International Gothic movement during the late 14th and 15th centuries. Stefano da Verona and Pisanello were among the most outstanding painters of this period, Pisanello being a particularly brilliant medallionist.

The Renaissance movement reached Verona rather later, in the mid-15th century, and with it came Andrea Mantegna, who had begun his painting career ten years earlier in Tuscany. From then on, all the painters working in Verona remained to a greater or lesser extent under the influence of Mantegna, until examples of Bellini's style and later of Giorgione and Titian started coming in from Venice. In the 14th and 15th centuries, Verona produced many famous artists, such as

Domenico and Francesco Morone, Liberale da Verona, Francesco Benaglio, Girolamo dai Libri, the two Caroto brothers, Francesco Bonsignori, Cavazzola, Nicolò Giolfino, Michele da Verona, to name but a few. Later artists include Francesco Torbido, Bonifacio de' Pitati, the two Brusasorcis, and Antonio Badile. During the late 16th century, the influence of Mannerism became visible in the work of Paolo Farinati, and in the work of others of the School of Verona. This was the period in which Verona gave Venice one of her most famous sons: one of the greatest painters of the century – Paolo Caliari, called "Veronese". Fra Giovanni, a monk belonging to the Order of the Mount of Olives, was responsible for the breathtaking wooden inlay work in the interiors of the

churches of Santa Maria in Organo, and Monteoliveto Maggiore, near Siena. The sculptor Antonio Rizzo did most of his best work in Venice, but the artist whose work is most remarkable in 16th century Verona is the military and civilian architect Michele Sanmicheli. He worked throughout the widespread Republic of Venice, spending a good deal of time in Verona. As well as being responsible for the walls which defended the city, Sanmicheli enriched the town with graceful palaces, imposing gateways, and his masterpiece, the Cappella Pellegrini.

During the Renaissance period many of Verona's sons distinguished themselves in the arts and sciences, such as Fra Giocondo, a philologist and an architect who is supposed to have designed the fine Loggia del Consiglio, as well as Guarino Guarini, Girolamo Fracastoro, a physician and a poet, G.C. Scaligero, Torello Saraina, Onofrio Panvinio, Giovanni Cotta, and the musician Antonio Ingegneri. During the Baroque period, there was a decline in the artistic activity of both Verona and Venice. There are however outstanding artists such as the architects Curtoni and Brugnoli and the painters Turchi, Bassetti and Balestra. Illustrious personages lived and worked in

▼ *Mullioned window and façade decorations of the Palazzo del Consiglio*

Verona during the 18th century when many Academies flourished. Mention should be made of Scipione Maffei, a great scholar and encyclopedist, scientists such as Noris and Lorgna, the architect Alessandro Pompei, a forerunner of Neoclassical art, Ignazio Pellegrini, engineer at the court of the Great Duke of Tuscany. Noteworthy painters are Giambettino Cignaroli, Rotari, Lorenzi, Marcola. Among the musicians, Evaristo Dall'Abaco, Giuseppe Torelli and Antonio Salieri are to be mentioned.

The arrival of Napoleon and the French and the fall of the Venetian Republic at the end of the 18th century brought an abrupt change in the history of Verona. Many decisive battles were fought in the area around

▼ *Panorama of downtown Verona at sunset*

the city, including those of Arcole and Rivoli. Against the invading Jacobins, the Veronese people, true to the traditions of Venice and Catholicism, rose in a rebellion known as the *Pasque Veronesi*, so called because it took place over Easter in April 1797. Thereafter, the town was captured by the Austrians and in 1801 it was split between Austria and France. In 1805, it became a part of the Kingdom of Italy, but finally returned under Austrian domination in 1814. This marked the beginning of a long and irksome subjection to Austria. This period was, however, punctuated by bold attempts at rebellion and conspiracies, which resulted in the death of patriots such as Carlo Montanari, born in Verona and hanged at Belfiore in March 1853. This period was also punctuated by important battles which took place in the neighbourhood of the city: the battles of Santa Lucia and Custoza in 1848, San Martino and Solferino, then the Peace of Villafranca in 1859, and a second battle of Custoza in 1866. Throughout this time there was much sacrifice and bloodshed, which only came to an end when the city finally became part of Italy again on the 16th October, 1866. Then began the long patient struggle to recover lost time and opportunities. Verona had to recover from the heavy military demands made upon it in the years of virtual bondage, when the city was the principal fortress of the Quadrilatero, a defensive system based on a square formation, with Verona, Peschiera, Mantua and Legnano at each corner. In 1882, it was flooded by the River Adige. In the years 1915-1918 it was in the front line of the First World War, and was among the most badly damaged of all Italian cities. During World War II Verona suffered severe bombing. Despite the natural and man-made disasters, Verona has emerged as one of the foremost cities in Italy, and looks forward to an increasingly prosperous future.

A brief glance at the culture and art of Verona during the 19th and 20th centuries shows that the town did not lag behind in modern developments and ideas. The 19th century saw the rise of poets such as Ippolito Pindemonte, Aleardo Aleardi and Antonio Cesari, architects such as Barbieri and Giuliari, sculptors like Della Torre and Fraccaroli, and painters such as Canella and Cabianca. The late 19th and early 20th centuries saw an upsurge of traditionalism in Veronese art.

► *Bird's eye view of the city*

The history of Verona has now reached modern times, and it is not necessary to mention a long list of important artists who are still living to prove that Verona still holds its own as an artistic and cultural centre.

Verona boasts numerous museums such as the Museum of Castelvecchio, the Archaeological Museum, the Natural History Museum, and a number of libraries among which the ancient Chapter Library, the Town Library, the Popular Library, as well as specialized university libraries. The Academy of Science and Letters, one of the most ancient and illustrious academies in Italy, hosts the Conservatory. Art galleries and exhibitions of contemporary art are also to be mentioned.

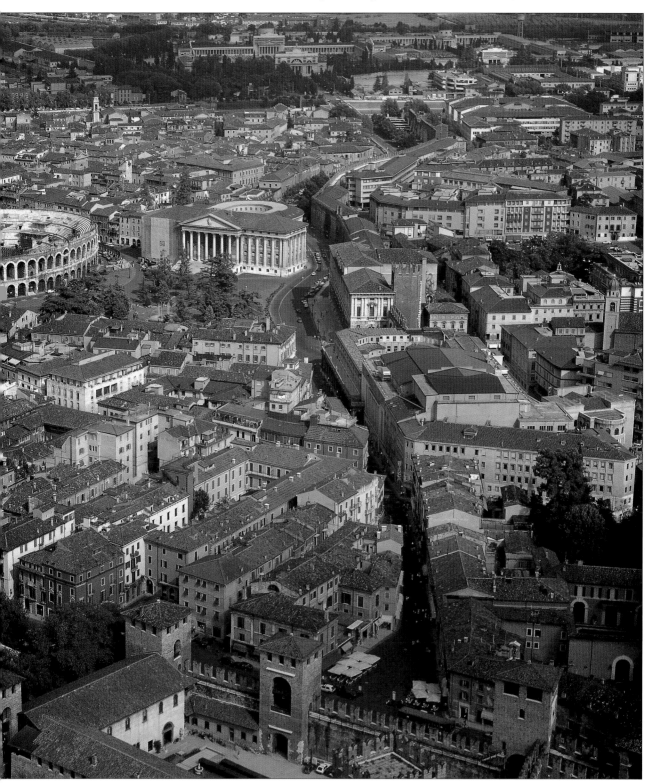

The most widely used and most convenient approaches to Verona are from the south, where the exits from the "Serenissima" and Brenner motorways and the junction of two main roads, the 11 and 12, are. The approach from this direction takes the visitor past the industrial area and the exhibition grounds, and the Porta Nuova railway station. The meeting place for the traffic converging on Verona from the south is the vast Porta Nuova square, just outside the circle of the walls built by the Venetians and the Austrians, which still surround the city. It is here that Verona really begins.

▲ ▼ *The Porta Nuova built by Sanmicheli in 1540. Side gateways are a later addition (1854)*

The massive **Porta Nuova**, through which the visitor enters this side of the city, is a monument to the genius of Michele Sanmicheli. The Porta Nuova was built between 1535 and 1540, but only part of what is now standing is original, as some of it was rebuilt by the Austrians in 1854. The Corso di Porta Nuova, flanked by modern buildings, leads directly to the city centre. In addition to the old towers and the surrounding hills, also the Prealps can be seen in the background.

PIAZZA BRA

▶ *Portoni della Bra and Torre Pentagona*

Piazza Bra is the largest square in Verona, in fact one of the most spacious and impressive in the whole of Italy. One enters the Piazza through a gateway known as the **Portoni della Bra**, consisting of two huge arches surmounted by battlements which formed part of the walls built by Gian Galeazzo Visconti at the end of the 14th century. This gateway is flanked on one side by the **Torre Pentagona**, which was also built at the end of the 14th century. The centre of Piazza Bra is occupied by public gardens, containing a statue erected in 1883 to *King Victor Emmanuel II*, as well as a more recent statue commemorating the *Partisan*.

▼ *Piazza Bra, equestrian monument to King Victor Emmanuel II*

▲ *Piazza Bra, the fountain*

*◀ ▼ 15th century shrine
of the Virgin near the Arena "Wing"*

▲ *Palazzo della Gran Guardia*

Many of the buildings on three sides of the square are of great architectural importance. The **Palazzo della Gran Guardia**, the first building on the left of the gateway, although similar in style to the work of Sanmicheli was built in 1610 by Domenico Curtoni. This palazzo, remained incomplete until 1820, is notable for its massive bulk, as well as the forceful design of the façade, the doorway, and the windows. After the Palazzo della Gran Guardia comes the Neoclassical **Palazzo Barbieri**, otherwise known as the "Nuova Gran Guardia" which now houses the town hall offices. It was built in 1838 by G. Barbieri in the then fashionable classical style. On the left is the **Amphitheatre**. The fourth side of the square has a gracefully

▲ *Palazzo Barbieri*

curving line of buildings, further emphasised by a very wide pavement, known as **Listone**, and it is here that many of the people of Verona like to take an evening stroll. Among these buildings, the **Palazzo Guastaverza** is noteworthy owing to its architecture designed by Sanmicheli.

▼ *The "Listone della Bra"*

MUSEO LAPIDARIO MAFFEIANO

This is reached through a passage under the arcade of Teatro Filarmonico, near the Portoni della Bra. Founded by the Veronese scholar Scipione Maffei in the first half of the 18th century, it is the oldest museum in Europe devoted to a collection of ancient inscriptions. In the open gallery, designed by A. Pompei, there is an outstanding exhibition of stone slabs bearing inscriptions, statues, funeral urns, and bas-reliefs, most of them Etruscan, Greek or Roman, with a few Medieval fragments. The collection was catalogued and described by Maffei himself in his publication *Museum Veronense*, 1749.

▲ *Entrance courtyard to the Museo Lapidario Maffeiano and the imposing pronaos of the Teatro Filarmonico*

▼ *Etruscan alabaster urn depicting Priam recognizing Paris*

▼ *Detail of a sarcophagus with Triton and Nereid (early 3rd cent. A.D.)*

▲ *Memorial stone with a winged putto*

Stone slab depicting dancing satyrs (2ⁿᵈ cent. A.D.) from San Zeno in Oratorio, formerly Temple of Bacchus

▼ *Marble relief with a Triton*

◀ *Funerary stele of husband and wife, Roman period*

▶ *Memorial stone of a Roman legionary*

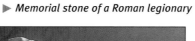

▲ ▶ *Funerary stele and relief*

THE ARENA

Fine Roman Amphitheatre, better known as the "Arena", is the most important of the monuments for which Verona is famed, and of which the city is so justly proud. Originally, the Amphitheatre stood outside the Roman walls of the city. In the 3rd century A.D., however, the Emperor Gallienus extended the latter to include the Arena, which is thought to have been built at the beginning of the 1st century In size and importance it is second only to the Colosseum in Rome. It covers an elliptical site measuring 456 feet by 360 feet, and the dimensions of the pit are 243 ft by 144 ft. The load-bearing structure consists of concrete and rubble with a facing of brick and stone from the quarries around Verona, and this combination of materials produces an attractive colour contrast. Very nearly the whole of the perimeter wall of the building has

▼ ▶ *The Roman Amphitheatre and the "Wing"*

▲ *Detail of the spans of the outer and inner elliptical walls*

disappeared, so that today all that remains is two tiers of arches built of rose coloured stone. Although it was never meant to be seen like this, the overall effect is extremely pleasing. In fact, most of the architecture in Verona built during the Renaissance was inspired by the Arena, the city's crowning glory. The perimeter wall fell into ruin or was deliberately destroyed over the centuries, and all that remains today is the fragment that towers above the arena, composed of three tiers with only four arches remaining on each tier. This is known to the people of Verona as the *Ala*, or wing.

The interior of the Arena is very impressive. From the pit, one looks up at flight upon flight of giant size terraces, which sweep upwards in

ever widening circles. The pride which the people of Verona take in this, the most famous of their monuments, is shown by the care lavished on the building. This pride first became evident in the late 16th century when a special council was set up, known as the *Conservatores Arenae*. This council was responsible for completely rebuilding the triple ring of internal arches supporting the terraces, and for the care of the 73 supports which radiate outwards and form the backbone of the structure.

The Amphitheatre of Verona served as a theatre for gladiatorial games, races, and other spectacular events; however, nowadays – actually from 1913 – the Arena is the regular setting for splendid operatic performances.

▲ ▼ *The Roman Amphitheatre and its imposing cavea*

▲ ▶ *Piazza delle Erbe and the so-called "Berlina",*
a 15th century shrine, the surrounding buildings,
the colourful market stalls and the ancient Domus Mercatorum

Piazza delle Erbe is more or less where the *Forum* of the Roman town was. The Piazza is one of the most picturesque in Italy. It epitomises the character and atmosphere of Verona, with its lively and colourful fruit and vegetable market, covered by its world-famous giant umbrellas, the delightful variety of styles of the surrounding buildings and its historically famous and centrally placed statues.

Starting from the south-western side of the square (from the corner of Via Mazzini), after the tall houses of the old Ghetto, one comes to a low building with its battlements and porticos. It was formerly the **Domus Mercatorum**, a magnificent Romanesque building, designed in 1301 by Alberto I della Scala, and extensively altered in the 19th century. At the far end of the square stands the impressive **Palazzo Maffei**, built in 1668, a dignified structure surmounted by a balustrade supporting six statues of mythical gods and goddesses (Hercules, Jupiter, Venus, Mercury, Apollo and Minerva). Apart from its beautiful statues, there is a lovely spiral staircase in the courtyard.

To the left of Palazzo Maffei, is the square, lofty bulk of the **Torre del Gardello**. Cansignorio della Scala had it built in brick in 1370 and the bell-shaped, battlemented belfry was completed in 1626.

On the north-east side, the first building is the picturesque **Casa Mazzanti**, decorated with frescoes of mythological subjects by A. Cavalli in the 16th century (recently restored). Next to the Casa Mazzanti

▲ *Piazza delle Erbe, Palazzo Maffei and the Torre del Gardello*

▲ The façade of Casa Mazzanti decorated with frescoes of mythological subjects

▼ The Lion of St. Mark and the balustrade of Palazzo Maffei in the background

is the **Domus Nova**, whose original design has been considerably altered over the years. After the "Arco della Costa", so called because of the whale rib which hangs beneath it, is the **Palazzo del Comune**. The Medieval facade on this side of the Palazzo was concealed in the 19th century by G. Barbieri, under a Neoclassical one. The Palazzo is flanked

▲ Detail of the wall paintings of Casa Mazzanti

▲ The Torre dei Lamberti and the side of Palazzo del Comune overlooking Piazza delle Erbe

▲ The whale rib hanging beneath the so-called Arco della Costa

▼ The Torre dei Lamberti topped by an octagonal belfry

by the **Torre dei Lamberti**, which rises 274 feet above the square, and is the tallest in Verona. It was begun in 1172 and completed in 1464 with the construction of the octagonal belfry, which still houses two ancient bells, the *Rengo* and the *Marangona*.

On the central island of the marble paved square, among the market stalls are several interesting statues. The first of them is a *Lion of St. Mark* on its 16th century column. The original sculpture was destroyed by the Jacobins in the 18th century but was replaced by a copy at the end of the 19th century. Then we come to the *Fountain of Madonna Verona*, which Cansignorio commissioned in 1368: a column decorated with heads and symbolic figures in relief and supporting a Roman statue rises out of a circular basin from which the water overflows into a wider and lower one. Next we come to a small, square, shrine-shaped construction once used during the ceremonies of investiture, when citizens were elected to public office. This building is commonly known as the **Berlina**.

Finally, at the edge of the "Toloneo", as the space occupied by the market is called, there is a pinnacled *aedicule* on a column (15th century).

The fountain of Madonna Verona (1368)

▲ *The column standing on the market square (1410)*

▶ *The plaque on the wall of Juliet's house*

QUESTE · FURONO · LE · CASE
DEI · CAPULETI
D'ONDE · USCÌ · LA · GIULIETTA
PER · CUI
TANTO · PIANSERO · I · CUORI · GENTILI
E · I · POETI · CANTARONO

SECOLI · 13 · E · 14 · E · V.

Verona is world famous as the setting for Skakespeare's Romeo and Juliet. Here the love story is brought vividly to life because quite a number of buildings mentioned in the play can still be seen

▼ *The legendary balcony of Juliet's house*

▲ *Bronze statue depicting Juliet, by N. Costantini*

in Verona today. **Juliet's House**, for instance, is in Via Cappello, not far from Piazza delle Erbe. It is a tall building, which probably dates back to the 13th century, with a mellow brick façade. Tradition in Verona has it that this was the house of the Capulets, the powerful Veronese family to which Juliet belonged.

From the inner courtyard, recently restored and around which the house is built, one can see the balcony which plays such an important part in the legend. Next to this balcony, some lines of Shakespeare's famous tragedy are engraved on a plaque in Italian and English.

▼ *Juliet's house*

▲ ▼ *Thanks to considerable renovation works, the interior of Juliet's house reproduces a typical 14th century setting. The two pictures refer to the large hall on the first floor and to the rooms on the second and third floor.*

PIAZZA DEI SIGNORI

Despite its proximity to Piazza delle Erbe, and the fact that it almost forms part of the same complex, Piazza dei Signori is totally different in shape, style and atmosphere. This Piazza was once described, somewhat romantically, as the "drawing room" of Verona, and it is true that it is probably the most distinguished and elegant place in the whole city, perhaps because of its peace and the harmony of the surrounding buildings.

Entering from Piazza delle Erbe, the **Palazzo del Comune** is on the right. The Romanesque façade of this tall building received considerable additions during the Renaissance period. It has the distinctive alternating bands of brick and stonework which can be considered the *leitmotiv* of the city as a whole. After a tall crenellated tower dating back to the second half of the 14th century is the **Palazzo del Capitano**, which has a 16th century façade, and a splendid entrance by Sanmicheli of the same century. In the courtyard stands the famous **Porta Bombardiera** built in 1687. The Piazza is bounded by the **Palazzo degli Scaligeri**, now the Prefecture. The original

▼ *Archway leading from the courtyard of the Courts of Justice to Piazza dei Signori*

▼ *Piazza dei Signori, the elegant walk of Verona*

building dates from the 12th century, but through the years it has been extensively altered. The façade itself, with its battlements in the style prevalent during the Ghibelline period, is the result of fairly recent restoration work. The *courtyard* is of particular interest, with its lovely Renaissance well, and with its *Gothic open gallery*, which used to be decorated with frescoes by Altichiero, painted in the 14th century. Both this Palazzo and the nearby Church of Santa Maria Antica have close associations with Dante, who found his "first refuge and welcome" in the home of the Scala family.

▼ *The elegant Loggia del Consiglio,
also named after "Fra Giocondo"*

▲ *The Domus Nova*

The most important monument in the Piazza dei Signori is the **Loggia del Consiglio**, built between 1476 and 1493. The attribution of the building to the Veronese architect Fra Giocondo is uncertain. This is the finest Renaissance building in Verona, where an almost Tuscan simplicity of lines blends with subtle decorative work and a warmth of colour reminiscent of Venetian architecture. Statues of *Catullus*, *Pliny*, *Marcus*, *Vitruvius*, and *Cornelius Nepos* by Alberto da Milano crown the building.

The 18th century façade of the **Domus Nova**, with its grand central arch, is on the other side of the Piazza. This building houses the *Caffè Dante*, which is unique in that it still maintains the original 19th century interior decoration. The statues of Enrico Noris, Scipione Maffei and Girolamo Fracastoro stand above the arches of the passageway. The *statue of Dante* standing in the centre of the square is the work of Ugo Zannoni, completed in 1865.

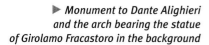

► *Monument to Dante Alighieri and the arch bearing the statue of Girolamo Fracastoro in the background*

▶ *The courtyard of the Mercato Vecchio*

This is the name given to the inner courtyard of the Palazzo del Comune, which one enters from the Piazza dei Signori, Piazza delle Erbe, and Via Cairoli. The inner walls of the square courtyard feature a striped decoration, obtained by using bands of brick and stone, common to both the exterior and interior walls. The courtyard is distinguished by the bold design of its gallery, which is built in the solid Romanesque style. The elegant Gothic staircase, its two flights supported on various kinds of arches, was added in the mid-15th century. The courtyard offers a splendid view of the Torre dei Lamberti; visitors can take the lift to reach the top of this tower.

▼ *Plaque used in ancient times for secret denunciations*

DENUNZIE SECRET
CONTRO USURARJ
E CONTRATI
USURATICI DI
QUALUNQUE SORTE

▶ *The stairway called Scala della Ragione is to be found in the courtyard of the Mercato Vecchio*

SANTA MARIA ANTICA AND THE SCALA TOMBS

The church of the Scala family was very near to their city mansion, and this is why they had their burial place built outside it.

This church was Santa Maria Antica, a very old one founded in the 7th century. Although it is small, the interior is very beautiful. It is a splendid example of Romanesque architecture in Verona, with a distinctive facing consisting of alternating bands of brick and stone on the outside, and cobbles included in the interior. The church tower is surmounted by a very fine square belfry, which has Gothic mullioned windows and a conical roof covered with tiles. Over the side-door there is the *tomb of Cangrande I della Scala*, who died in 1329. This also serves as a porch and is one of the best examples of 14th century sculpture in Verona. Under a Gothic canopy, supported by columns and topped by a pyramid shaped roof is the sarcophagus, decorated with sculpture in high relief. The statue of the dead prince lies on top of his tomb on a couch. This monument is unique, however, because of the *statue of Cangrande on horseback* which stands on top of its

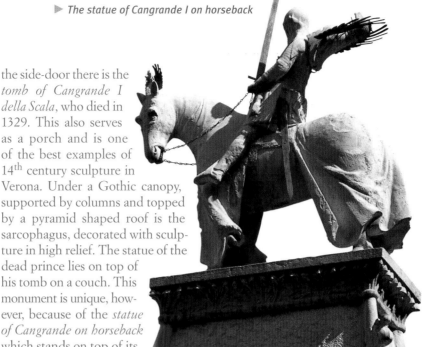

▶ *The statue of Cangrande I on horseback*

▼ *The Scala family tombs and the church of Santa Maria Antica*

▲ *A detail of the tomb of Mastino II and the bell tower of Santa Maria Antica*

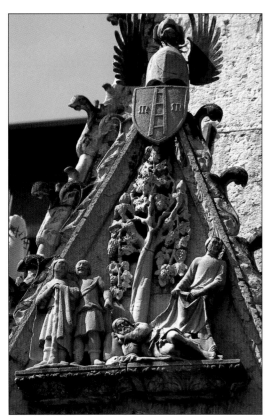

▲ *Tomb of Mastino II: detail of the sculpture depicting Noah's drunkenness*

pyramid roof. It is the masterpiece of an anonymous sculptor of the 14th century known as the "Maestro delle Arche Scaligere". This sculptor has portrayed the smiling horseman in vigorous and realistic style on his alert steed caparisoned for tournament. The original statue is now in the Castelvecchio Museum. The monument to Cangrande is the only one outside the marble enclosure with its splendid wrought-iron fence, which bears the crest of the Scala family. All the other tombs are within the enclosed area, many in the shape of a sarcophagus set on the ground. One of the latter is the *tomb of Giovanni delle Scala* (who died in 1359) by Venetian stonemasons. Next to the entrance gate stands the *monument to Mastino II*, built between 1340 and 1350. It is raised on columns, and, like the earlier monument to Cangrande, the tomb lies under a Gothic canopy with decorated finials, surrounded by four small aedicules, its pyramid crowned by the statue of the prince on horseback. The tomb is carved in high relief with figures of angels at each corner.

We now come to the most ornate of all the Scala family tombs – that of *Cansignorio*, died in 1375. It is by Bonino da Campione and Gaspare Broaspini, and although it is based on the same architectural plan as the others, the workmanship is superior. The ornate decorations on the canopy were sculpted with remarkable skill and delicacy, so that the end result is like an immense and intricately elaborate ivory carving. The side aedicules are particularly remarkable as well as the work on the tomb itself. The Scala funeral monuments are the supreme Gothic art achievement in Verona.

▼ *Equestrian monument to Mastino II*

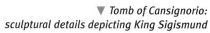

▼ Equestrian statue
of Cansignorio

▲ The tomb of Cansignorio, by Bonino da Campione and Gaspare Broaspini

ROMEO'S HOUSE

This fine Medieval building, in Via delle Arche Scaligere, is popularly identified with the House of the Montecchi, or Montagues, Romeo's family.

The house is built of brick, and there are still traces of the original battlements, although it is now in such bad condition that no visitors are allowed into the inner courtyard.

◄ *Romeo's house,*
Via delle Arche Scaligere

MODERN ART GALLERY

The beautiful Palazzo Forti (formerly Palazzo Emilei), was designed by Ignazio Pellegrini at the end of the 18th century. Recent restoration has brought to light important traces of the 13th century *Palazzo di Ezzelino*, which once stood on the site.

Today, the building houses the *Modern and Contemporary Art Gallery "Achille Forti"*, where the ground floor is mainly used for special exhibitions, chiefly devoted to contemporary or modern art, whereas the beautiful rooms upstairs are generally occupied by a series of 19th and

20th centuries local artists' works which have not yet been assigned a definite position and are thus exhibited in rotation in these rooms. This building used to house the Museum of the Risorgimento, now no longer in existence.

SANT'ANASTASIA

The largest church in Verona was founded by the Dominicans in 1290 and completed in 1481. It is built on the site of an older and much smaller church likewise dedicated to St. Anastasia, of which nothing remains save the name. The facing on the lofty façade is unfinished and only covers the lower portion of the building on each side of the impressive portal. Access to the church is through the mullioned twin-Gothic arched doorway. The doors are framed by gracefully fluted narrow pilasters of variously coloured marble rising to form a Gothic arch above the mullioned aperture. The carving on the architrave dates from the 14th century and resembles the decorative

▼ *View of Sant'Anastasia from the hill of San Pietro*

▲ *Night view of the church of Sant'Anastasia*

work on the Scala family tombs. The frescoes above, however, date from the early 15th century and are much deteriorated. The bas-reliefs on the right pillar, representing *Episodes from the Life of St. Peter the Martyr*, are 15th century too.

The church possesses a high, mellow brick bell tower built in the 15th century.

▼ *Reliefs on the right pillar featuring the Sermon and the Death of Saint Peter the Martyr*

▲ ▼ *The façade of Sant'Anastasia and the outstanding mullioned doorway*

▲ *The majestic interior of the church of Sant'Anastasia*

1565. The second chapel dedicated to *St. Vincent Ferrer*, and attributed to Pietro da Porlezza, contains delicate marble relief work. On the upper part of the wall there is a 15th century fresco while the altarpiece, portraying *St. Vincent Ferrer*, is by P. Rotari (18th century) The third chapel is designed on the same plan as the preceding one and the lunette contains a painting of the *Descent from the Cross* by Liberale da Verona, dating from the 15th century. The fourth chapel is reminiscent of Verona's Roman Arch of the Gavii. The altarpiece shows *St. Martin* painted by F. Caroto, and the painting of *Mary Magdalene* above it is by Liberale. The sixth chapel is known as the *chapel of the Crucifixion*. The bas-relief decoration is by P. da Porlezza. It contains the *Funeral monument to Gianesello da*

▲ ▶ The famous holy water stoups referred to as the "Hunchbacks" of Sant'Anastasia

INTERIOR. One of the most outstanding examples of Gothic church architecture in Verona. All the craftsmen were local. Its proportions and various elements of its design, however, are still markedly Romanesque. The stylised paintings of plants which decorate the dome are worthy of note The floor was designed by Pietro da Porlezza in 1462. In front of the first column facing the nave are *holy water stoups* supported by human figures in a crouched sitting position, known as the *"Hunchbacks"* of St. Anastasia.

RIGHT AISLE. The first altar, commissioned by the *Fregoso Family*, was designed by Danese Cattaneo in

Folgaria (about 1425) and a *Pietà*, with figures in painted stone. At the end of the right *transept* is the beautiful *altar* dedicated to *St. Thomas Aquinas*. The altarpiece is by Girolamo dei Libri, and shows a *Madonna and Child with Saints*.

TRANSEPT. It houses five altars, including the high altar. The first chapel on the right, known as the Cavalli Chapel (*Cappella Cavalli*), contains the only non-fragmentary fresco in Verona which can be attributed with certainty to Altichiero; the mural is therefore of great interest and shows the *Cavalli Family before the Virgin*. It was painted around 1390. The frescoes on the pillar and the one in the lunette above the *Tomb of Federico Cavalli* date from the early 15th century and are by Martino da Verona. *St. George freeing the Princess from the Dragon*, Pisanello's most famous fresco, used to be above the arch of the second chapel in the transept, known as the *Cappella Pellegrini*. (It is now in the sacristy to the left of the transept). The walls of the chapel are completely covered with terracotta panels depicting *Scenes from the Life of Christ*, the most important work of Michele da Firenze dating from 1435.

The elegant Gothic *Sanctuary* contains the 14th century fresco of the *Last Judgement* on the right hand wall, and the impressive *Tomb of Cortesia Serègo* built in 1424-1429. This tomb is surrounded by an outstanding fresco depicting the *Annunciation* in the International Gothic style, attributed to Michele Giambono. Also to be seen are the Lavagoli chapel decorated with with 15th century frescoes taking inspiration from Mantegna, and the Salerni chapel, with the funeral monument to Giovanni Salerni dating from the 15th century, and fresco of the same period. Noteworthy is the 14th century wall painting at the end of the transept wall, on either side of the doorway to the sacristy.

◀ *Madonna Enthroned and Saints Augustine and Thomas Aquinas, by Girolamo dai Libri*

▲ *Saint George freeing the Princess, by Pisanello*

▲ *The Madonna of the Rosary, a 14ᵗʰ century panel painting*

LEFT AISLE. The *Rosary Chapel* is built in lavish late 16ᵗʰ century style and contains paintings and sculpture by local artists of the Baroque era. Over the altar, 14ᵗʰ century panel painting of the *Madonna of the Rosary*, protector of the town. The *organ* and the *gallery* date to 1625. Next comes the *Miniscalchi Chapel* (16ᵗʰ century); the *lunette* fresco is by Francesco Morone and the panel painting of the *Pentecost* is by N. Giolfino (16ᵗʰ century).

The third altar on the left (at the entrance) is dedicated to *St. Raymond*, and the altarpiece is a *Madonna and Saints* by D. Brusasorci (16ᵗʰ century). The second altar on the left is dedicated to *St. Erasmus*, and the altar-

piece is *Christ and Saints* by Nicolò Giolfino. First altar to the left (*Boldieri Chapel*): Renaissance architecture with niches and polychrome-stone statues reminiscent of those in the central polyptych. The frescoes attributed to F. Morone depict the *Virgin* and *Saint John the Evangelist*.

The *Tomb of Guglielmo di Castelbarco* stands in the Piazza di Sant'Anastasia on the left of the façade as one faces the church. It was built around 1320, and anticipates the suspended structure of the Scala family tombs. A side of the little square is the wall of the **church of San Pietro Martire**, built in the 14ᵗʰ century, usually closed to visitors.

The interior is decorated with frescoes and coats of arms of the *Brandeburger Knights*. The *tomb of Bavarino Crescenzi* can be seen on the façade.

◀ *Tomb of Guglielmo di Castelbarco*

THE CATHEDRAL

Santa Maria Matricolare, the Cathedral of Verona, stands in a small square flanked by ancient buildings, which create a perfect setting for the lovely old church, that was partly built on the site of a very ancient pre-existing basilica. It was consecrated in 1187, although building and decoration continued long after this date.

The design of the façade is unusual because of the mixture of Romanesque and Gothic elements. There is a splendid *canopy* above

▼ *The massive Cathedral building soaring aloft in the sky*

▲ *Detail of the lunette depicting the Adoration of the Magi*

◀ ▲ *The façade of the Cathedral and the magnificent double-arched porch*

the doorway, composed of two arches, one above the other. It is an example of the Romanesque style developed in Verona and the Po Valley, ascribed to Master Nicolò and his school, who built the entrance in 1138. The right hand side of the building, the only one completely visible, is of great interest, with its lovely side door, as is also the **apse** with its excellent relief work executed by Veronese craftsmen. The bell tower is not complete, despite work carried out recently by the architect E. Fagiuoli. The 16th century middle section is by Sanmicheli.

▲ Column-bearing griffin to the right of the doorway

◀ Sculptural detail of the portal embrasure featuring the Prophets

▼ Column details, column-bearing lion and a frieze
depicting a dragon decorating the upper portion of the canopy

▲ A capital with a "Hunchback"

▼ *Capital and lintel of the side porch featuring the story of Jonas and the Whale*

▼ *Lane to the left of the Cathedral leading to Sant'Elena; the sarcophagus in the foreground bears witness to the ancient churchyard*

▲ *The porch on the right hand side of the cathedral*

◀ *Relief with a lion decorating a capital of the side porch*

▲ *Interior of the Cathedral*

INTERIOR. Spacious and impressive. Two lines of powerfully ribbed piers branch out to support the Gothic vaulting, dividing the nave from the aisles. The trompe-l'oeil architecture scenes painted in the first three chapels in both right and left aisles is by G. M. Falconetto and date from the 16th century.

RIGHT AISLE. The second chapel contains the *Adoration of the Magi* by Liberale da Verona, and the *Descent from the Cross, with Four Saints* by N. Giolfino. The third chapel houses the 18th century *Transfiguration* by G. B. Cignaroli and the *death mask of Pope Lucius III*, (died 1185). At the end of the right aisle, in the Cappella Mazzanti, lies the **Tomb of Saint Agatha**, a masterpiece by a follower of Bonino da Campione, dated 1353. The church's *sanctuary* contains remarkable frescoes painted in the dome of the apse and on the arch. The subjects are the *Annunciation*, and the *Stories of Mary and the Prophets*, painted by F. Torbido in the 16th century from sketches by Giulio Romano.

A marble choir screen by Sanmicheli encloses the sanctuary.

LEFT AISLE. Fourth chapel: *Our Lady of Mercy*, a painting from the 16th century, mainly remade in the 18th century. The third chapel contains the *Madonna*

▶ *The Assumption by Titian*

and Saints by A. Brenzoni (1533), and the *Epitaph of Archdeacon Pacifico*, a famous Veronese personage of the 9th century. The first (*Nichesola*) Chapel, with carved decorations by the famous Venetian architect Sansovino, contains the famous altarpiece by Titian (ca. 1530), the *Assumption* (the only painting he actually worked on in Verona). To the left of the entrance is the *Nichesola Monument*, an important work by Jacopo Sansovino.

▲ ▶ *Gallery with coupled columns of the old Chapter cloister onto which the famous Chapter Library opens (entrance from Piazza del Duomo), containing a collection of illuminated manuscripts and other valuable documents*

SAN GIOVANNI IN FONTE

This small church, the former Baptistery of the Cathedral, was founded around the 8th-9th centuries. The existing structure including a nave, two aisles and three apses, dates from the early 12th century. Only the capitals of the columns of the earlier structure are still extant.

▲ *Relief of the baptismal font and depicting the Annunciation*

INTERIOR. The church contains paintings by local artists of the 16th century as well as the remains of 13th, 14th and 15th cent. frescoes. The magnificent octagonal *Baptismal Font* (ca. 1200), one of the most outstanding examples of Medieval Veronese sculpture, stands in the centre. It is made of a single block of pink marble and around the exterior of each of the eight sides of the font are bas-reliefs with scenes from the New Testament, six of which, from the *Annunciation to the Shepherds* to the *Baptism of Christ*, bear a close resemblance to the style of Maestro Brioloto in his sculptures on the façade of San Zeno. The remaining two panels, depicting the *Annunciation* and *Visitation*, and the *Nativity*, are by another hand, although in Venetian Byzantine style.

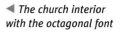

◄ *The church interior with the octagonal font*

PALAZZO VESCOVILE

The Bishop's Palace has a 16th century façade and battlements. Over the entrance stand statues of *Saints Michael*, *Peter* and *Paul*, and in the lunette is a painting of the *Madonna and Child* attributed to Fra Giovanni da Verona. The *courtyard* is a pastiche of styles from various centuries, and faces the apses of San Giovanni in Fonte. The crenellated tower dates from 1172. The statue of *David* is by A. Vittoria (16th century) The walls of the *Salone dei Vescovi* (Hall of the Bishops) are covered with 16th century frescoes by D. Brusasorci.

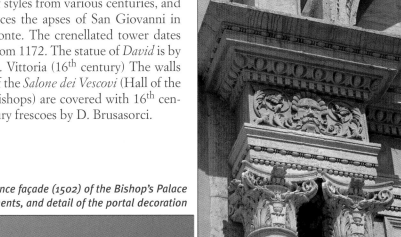

▼ ▶ *Renaissance façade (1502) of the Bishop's Palace crowned with Venetian battlements, and detail of the portal decoration*

CHURCH OF SANT'EUFEMIA

This great church, begun in 1275, and was eventually consecrated in 1331, but its original structure was greatly altered throughout the following centuries. The fine portal is 15th century, and there are two tall double windows. On the façade is the marble sarcophagus and the *Tomb of the Lavagnoli Family* (ca. 1550). On the left, there is the *Verità Family Tomb*. The bell tower is Romanesque in style.

INTERIOR. There is a central nave with ceiling decorated with modern frescoes. Second altar on the right: altarpiece by F. Torbido showing *Saints Barbara*, *Anthony Abbot* and *Roch* (16th century). The third altar on the right is decorated with a *Madonna and Six Saints* by D. Brusasorci. Seventh altar on the right: *Madonna and Saint Thomas of Villanova* by Cignaroli (18th century). The *Chapel of the Spolverini dal Verme Family* is decorated with frescoes depicting the *Voyage of Tobias*,

▲ *The façade of Sant'Eufemia*

▼ *The interior of Sant'Eufemia*

St. Ursula and *St. Lucy*, by F. Caroto. On the left wall *Madonna and Saints* by Moretto da Brescia, and the *Crucifixion* by F. Brusasorci. A fresco of Stefano da Verona (14th cent.) depicting *Saint Augustine*, in very bad condition, was recently removed from the outer lunette over the left gate and displayed in the church interior.

PORTA BORSARI

This archway stands at the end of Corso Porta Borsari, and was the *decuman gate* of the Roman city. All one can see of the gate today is the façade, which faces towards Corso Cavour, as the building itself has now collapsed. This remnant of Roman Verona is next in importance to the Amphitheatre, and dates from the second half of the 1st century. The gateway, which formed part of the first circle of city walls, consists of the two original arches with their lintels, tympana, and columns, surmounted by a double row of windows. The decoration on these windows inspired the architects of the Renaissance period, from Sanmicheli onwards. The gate bears an inscription dating to 245 A.D. in which Verona is given its Roman name: COLONIA VERONA AUGUSTA.

▼ ▶ *Porta Borsari, with two archways, stands at the end of the ancient* decumanus maximus

▲ *Detail of a triangular tympanum with an inscription bearing witness to the construction of the gate at time of Emperor Gallienus*

THE PALAZZI ON CORSO CAVOUR

I n Roman times Corso Cavour was the *Via Sacra* located outside the city walls.

LEFT SIDE. The 16th century **Palazzo Carnesali**, a well-proportioned building with elegant doorways and balconies. **Palazzo Scannagatti-Gobetti** is a fine example of Renaissance architecture in Verona, with

▲ *Palazzo Bevilacqua,*
detail of the façade decoration

▼ *Palazzo Canossa,*
by Sanmicheli (ca. 1530) with a loggia
and statues added in the 18th century

fine balconies and good relief decoration in marble. **Palazzo Bevilacqua** is one of Michele Sanmicheli's masterpieces, dating from about 1530. It is thought to have formed part of a project which was never completed by the architect.

RIGHT SIDE. The impressive **Palazzo Carlotti**, dating from 1665, designed by P. Schiavi. The Neoclassical **Palazzo Portalupi** (1802), by the architect G. Pinter, now seat of the Banca d'Italia. The small **Palazzo Muselli** is an elegant example of the Baroque, distinguished by its tall chimneys in Medieval style. **Palazzo Canossa** was built to a classical design by Sanmicheli around 1530, and the loggia and statues were added in the 18th century, together with the spacious courtyard overlooking the River Adige. The interior was decorated with great frescoes by Tiepolo depicting the *Glory of Hercules*, destroyed during World War II.

CHURCH OF SAN LORENZO

This is one of the most beautiful and important churches in Verona. It is built on the site of an Early Christian basilica, some fragments of which are visible from the courtyard. One enters the courtyard from Corso Cavour, passing under an archway bearing a statue of St. Laurence. It was built about 1117 and soon afterwards considerably enlarged.

The exterior is in typical Romanesque style, with alternating bands of brick and stone. The porch on the right and the bell tower, which was restored quite recently, were both originally built in the second half of the 15th century. The church has a unique feature: the two *cylindrical towers* housing the spiral staircases leading up to the women's galleries.

INTERIOR. This is one of the best examples of pure Romanesque style

▶ *Gothic archway with the statue of St. Laurence (1476); entrance to the side courtyard of the church*

in Verona. There is a peaceful, silent atmosphere and the severity of the design is only lightened by the effect of the alternating bands of stone and brick. The graceful arches and women's gallery are supported by lofty and well-proportioned piers. Fragments of 13th century frescoes on the walls include huge *St. Christopher*. Over the altar is a *Madonna and Saints* by D. Bru-

sasorci, and on the left are 16th century sarcophagi.

◀ *Side entrance with a Renaissance porch (ca. 1477) and view of a tower of the ancient façade*

▲ *The interior of San Lorenzo*

ARCH OF THE GAVII

▶ *The Arch of the Gavii*
(Ist century A.D.)

This arch stands in a small square overlooking the River Adige at the end of Corso Cavour, to which it was moved in 1930. Originally, it stood in the middle of the busy thoroughfare, near the clock tower of the Castelvecchio, from where it was removed and incorporated in the medieval city walls. It was broken up by the French in 1805.

▼ *Detail of the decorative columns of the arch*

▶ *Frieze decorating the front of the arching*

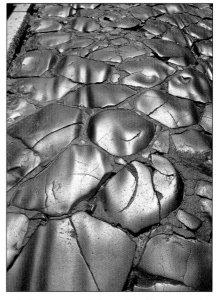

▲ *Flagstones of the ancient Roman paving beneath the Arch of the Gavii*

CASTELVECCHIO

▲ *Castelvecchio seen from the banks of the Adige*

The massive and crenellated Castelvecchio (literally the Old Castle), formerly known as the Castello di San Martino, was built as a stronghold by Cangrande II della Scala during the years 1354-55. Incorporated in its structure was an extensive portion of the city walls, terminating at the River Adige. The castle has had a fairly eventful history as it has survived, though not unscathed, successive dominations by various ruling families, plus the Venetians, French and Austrians. The small fort in the inner courtyard was built by Napoleon. For obvious military reasons the castle battlements and towers were cut down, not to be restored until the third decade of the 20th century, when the ancient fortress was given a new role as a museum.

▶ *External view of Castelvecchio with its massive towers and the gateway leading to the bridge on the River Adige*

▲ *Main view of the fortified walls, and the entrance facing the city*

▲ *Gallery, balconies and Gothic Venetian loggia giving onto the garden of the former stronghold*

◄ *The ancient drawbridge*

The irregular line of the external walls is punctuated by six roofed towers, one of which, taller and more strongly fortified than the others, is known as the **Mastio** (keep). The castle walls are bounded by a deep moat through which flowed the so-called "Adigetto" (or little Adige). The interior is divided by partition walls which separate it into three courtyards of varying sizes. Recent excavation has unearthed some interesting remains of the castle as it originally was, such as the

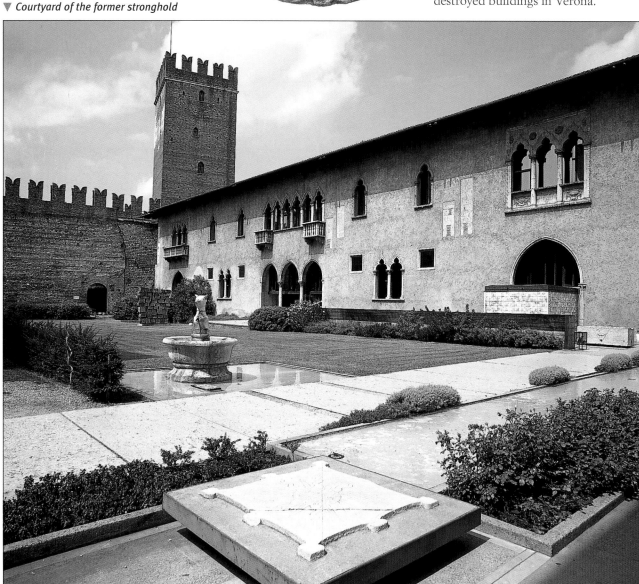

◀ *Pietra dura inlaid work pertaining to Della Scala family, to be seen in the courtyard beside the entrance to the Museum.*

Morbio Postern Gate, part of the inner ramparts, and the remains of the tiny and ancient church of San Martino. The fort built under Napoleon's rule underwent considerable changes between 1923 and 1926 when it was restored. At this time, new architectural elements were introduced in the façade, mainly jambs of doorways and windows from ancient destroyed buildings in Verona.

▼ *Courtyard of the former stronghold*

▶ *The sarcophagus of Saints Sergius and Bacchus bearing the date of 1179*

The buildings of Castelvecchio have been almost fully and radically restored to their original form thanks to restoration work begun in 1958 and terminated in 1964 (Carlo Scarpa, L. Magagnato). The rigorous interior layout and the museum outfitting have turned the old art collections into one of the most advanced and appealing museums in the whole of Europe. The visit to the rooms begins on the ground floor, where the curator's office and the library are located.

◀ *14th century Veronese sculptures depicting St. Catherine of Alexandria, St. Cecilia and St. Martha*

ROOM 1. Romanesque sculpture influenced by the Veronese style. *Sarcophagus of Saints Sergius and Bacchus* (1179), 13th century *Male figure* attributed to Brioloto; 12th century *Female figures supporting a stone slab*; ciborium front panels and slabs. The modern annex to this room in the shape of a small apse houses a precious collection of Longobard jewellery, early Medieval gold, bronze and glass items.

ROOM 2. 14th century Veronese sculpture, including the statues of *Saints Catherine of Alexandria, Cecilia, Martha* and *John the Baptist* (from the church of San Giacomo di Tomba).

ROOM 3. 14th century Veronese sculpture, including a *Madonna and Child Enthroned*, a *Crucifixion*, a *Madonna* and *Saint Libera*.

▲ ▶ *Crucifixion and St. Libera,*
examples of 14th century Veronese sculpture

▲ *Crucifixion featuring the Virgin and St. John the Evangelist,*
from the church of San Giacomo di Tomba

▼ *St. Martin and the Poor (1436)*

▲ *Fainting Madonna,*
by the Master of Sant'Anastasia

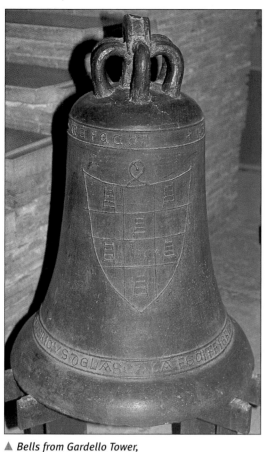

ROOM 4. 14th century Veronese sculpture. To be noted are the expressive *Crucifixion* from the church of San Giacomo di Tomba and the *Fainting Madonna* by the Master of Sant'Anastasia.

ROOM 5. Late 15th century sculpture, including panels with *Prophets*, *St. Peter Enthroned* and *St. Martin and the Poor.*

A large bell bearing the mark of Master Jacopo (1370) can be seen at the end of the sculpture gallery. Once it stood on the Gardello Tower, Piazza delle Erbe.

The **Morbio Postern Gate** built in the ancient city walls dating back to the times of the Commune leads to the Main Tower and to the other rooms.

ROOM 6. (Beyond the defensive wall): ancient *Bells of Verona* (14th-16th cent.).

Here is the entrance to the portion of Castelvecchio known as the "Reggia" or Royal Hall, which is still the best preserved section.

ROOM 7. (First floor): 13th and 14th century frescoes from churches and buildings in Verona. Fine 14th century jewellery can be seen in a glass case.

ROOM 8. Detached 14th century frescoes by Veronese artists (*Madonna and Child*, *Coronation of the Virgin* from the sarcophagus of Aventino Fracastoro, *Crucifixion*, to name just a few).

ROOM 9. *Polyptych of the Holy Trinity* by Turone di Maxio (1360), a 14th century altar-frontal by an anonymous artist depicting *Sain Catherine* and a *Crucifixion, Saints and a Nun* by Tommaso da Modena, and the *Boi Family Polyptych* by the followers of Altichiero.

ROOM 10. This section of "international" Gothic painting is one of the outstanding collections in the museum, with works by late Gothic masters including the *Madonna of Humility* and *Saint Jerome in the Desert* by Jacopo Bellini; the charming *Madonna of the Quail* by Pisanello, the *Nursing Madonna* by Michele Giambono, the *Madonna of the Rose*

▲ *Bells from Gardello Tower, cast by Master Jacopo in 1370*

▼ *Polyptych of the Holy Trinity, by Turone*

▲ *Madonna of the Rose Garden, by Stefano da Verona*

Garden and a *Madonna and Child* by Stefano da Verona; *Christ in the Sepulchre* attributed to Domenico Veneziano; an early 15th century *Adoration of the Magi* by an unknown Paduan artist. A number of precious *miniatures* is also on display.

ROOM 11. 14th and 15th centuries sculpture and paintings, including the *Death of the Virgin* by Giambono, a *Crucifixion* by Jacopo Bellini; the *Aquila Polyptych* and the *Fracanzani Altarpiece* by Giovanni Badile. In addition, the *Altarpiece* from the convent of San Bartolomeo della Levata, two *Polyptychs* by the so-called Maestro del Cespo di Garofano and two *Processional Crosses* by a 14th century Veronese artist.

ROOM 12. Dedicated to the works of foreign artists, among them Peter Paul Rubens, Marten van Cleef, Hans de Jode, Joachim Beuckelaer, Konrad Faber von Kreuznach, Ambrosius Benson, Herri met de Bles known as "Civetta" (Owl) and William Key.

▲ *St. Blaise and a Saint Bishop, by Bartolomeo Montagna*

▼ *Detail of the Madonna in Adoration, by Francesco Bonsignori*

ROOM 13. (Second floor of the Royal Hall): Venetian masters of the Renaissance, in particular Giovanni Bellini, with two paintings of the *Madonna and Child*, Vittore Carpaccio's *Two Female Saints with a Page*, Bartolomeo Montagna's *Saint Blaise and a Saint Bishop*, and other paintings including works by Alvise Vivarini and Giovanni Mansueti.

ROOM 14. Important works by Veronese Renaissance painters, namely Domenico and Francesco Morone.

▲ ◄ The Sambonifacio Dower Chest, by Liberale da Verona, depicting the Triumph of Chastity and the Triumph of Love

ROOM 15. Outstanding paintings by Francesco Bonsignori (*Allegory of Music*, *Dal Bovo Madonna* and *Madonna in Adoration*), as well as a work by Antonio Vivarini (*Saint Christopher*).

ROOM 16. Dedicated primarily to Liberale da Verona, this room houses his *Nativity and Saint Jerome*, the *Sambonifacio Dower Chest*, the *Madonna of the Goldfinch*, and a *Deposition from the Cross*.

ROOM 17. This is the central stateroom on the second floor of the Royal Hall housing frescoes and outstanding paintings on panel by Nicola Giolfino, Domenico Morone, Giovanni Maria Falconetto, Liberale da Verona and Francesco Verla.

ROOM 18. Paintings by Andrea Mantegna: *Christ Carrying the Cross*, the *Holy Family and a Saint*, *Madonna and Child with St. Margaret* by Francesco Bonsignori, *Madonna and Child* known as *Madonna della Passione* by Carlo Crivelli, as well as works by Domenico Morone, Francesco Benaglio and Jacopo da Valenza.

ROOM 19. (Next to the Keep) Ancient arms (Da Prato Collection) and a *Portrait of Pase Guarienti* attributed to Battista del Moro.

An open passageway leads back into the main museum building, past the concrete plinth with the original of the superb *Equestrian Statue of Cangrande I* (from the funeral monuments of the Scala Family).

▲ *The Holy Family and a Female Saint, by Andrea Mantegna*

▲ *The original equestrian statue of Cangrande I, from the Scala family tombs*

▲ *Portrait of a Child with a Drawing,*
by Giovan Francesco Caroto

ROOM 20. Great *Polyptych of the Passion* by Paolo Morando known as Cavazzola, *Incredulity of Saint Thomas* also by Cavazzola, as well as other paintings. In addition, two charming paintings on panel by Giovan Francesco Caroto can also be seen: *Young Benedictine Monk* and *Child with a Drawing*.

ROOM 21. Devoted to works by G. F. Caroto and Girolamo dai Libri, in particular the *Nativity with Rabbits* by this latter artist.

ROOM 22. Works by major 16th century Venetian artists: *Deposition* and *Bevilacqua Lazise Altarpiece* by Veronese; *Adoration of the Shepherds* and *Contest between the Muses and the Pierides* by Jacopo Tintoretto.

ROOM 23. 16th and 17th century Mannerist painters such as Paolo Farinati, Domenico Brusasorci, Francesco Maffei, Pasquale Ottino, Alessandro Turchi, Orlando Flacco and Jacopo Palma the Younger.

ROOM 24. Interesting 17th century Veronese paintings, especially works by Marcantonio Bassetti, Bernardo Strozzi, and others.

ROOM 25. 17th century paintings including works by Alessandro Turchi, Giovan Benedetto Castiglione, Bernardo Strozzi, Claudio Ridolfi, etc.

ROOM 26. 18th century paintings. *Four Camaldolensian Saints* and the *Sketch for a Ceiling of Ca' Rezzonico* by Giandomenico Tiepolo, a *Story of the Maccabees* by Giambattista Tiepolo, two splendid *Capricci* by Francesco Guardi, *Coffee Time* by Pietro Longhi, *Bacchus and Ariadne* by Luca Giordano. Works by Antonio Balestra, Mattia Preti and Giambettino Cignaroli are also on display.

▼ *Deposition from the Cross, by Veronese*

▲ *Sketch for a ceiling of Ca' Rezzonico, by Giandomenico Tiepolo*

▲ *Capriccio, by Francesco Guardi*

PONTE SCALIGERO

This famous bridge (named after the Scala family) forms part of the complex defence system of Castelvecchio. Although its original purpose was merely military, it is nevertheless a masterpiece of Medieval design and engineering.

Built in 1355 under Cangrande II della Scala, its architect has been identified as Guglielmo Be-

vilacqua. The bridge has three great arches supported by solid turreted pylons – the widest boasting a 160 ft. span. Both the arches and the towers as well as the tall swallow-tail battlements are chiefly built in brick.

The bridge presents a very imposing sight, with its glowing red brick, and the interior is no less impressive, giving fine views over the river and the city. Over the

centuries, it was altered in many ways, and during the World War II it was almost totally destroyed. However, reconstruction began immediately, and the bridge is now restored to its original splendour.

► *A night view of the bridge and the complex of Castelvecchio*

▼ *The Ponte Scaligero*

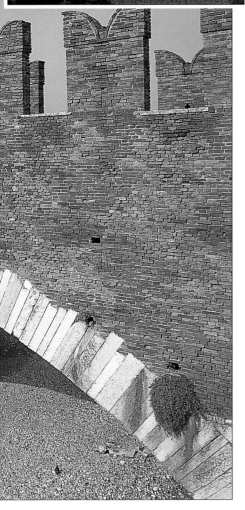

▲ *Communication trench of the bridge overshadowed by the huge Keep*

CHURCH OF SAN ZENO MAGGIORE

The Basilica of San Zeno Maggiore ranks, together with the Amphitheatre, as one of Verona's outstanding monuments. It is considered one of the great achievements of Romanesque architecture. The present building is the third Basilica built on the same site. The first church was built in the 4th-5th centuries, the second in the 10th century. The present church was commenced around 1120; shortly afterwards, the builders started enlarging it and work continued until the end of the 14th century. The roof and the apse were rebuilt in the Gothic period.

◀ *The rose window of San Zeno decorated with the symbols of Fortune, by Master Brioloto*

▼ *The Basilica of San Zeno Maggiore with its splendid bell tower and the 13th century tower*

FAÇADE. The splendid façade is perhaps the most outstanding of this period. It dominates an enormous paved square, and is flanked by a beautiful Romanesque *bell tower* from the first half of the 12th century, of superbly masterful design. On the other side stands the red 12th century *tower* of the ancient monastery mentioned by Dante in Canto 18 of his "Purgatory". The weathered Veronese stone of which the church is built has a warm golden tone, and the restrained lines of the pillars, the columns, the cornices and the gallery with its double windows give the whole façade an air of harmonious elegance. The front of the building is crowned with a tympanum decorated with marble columns, and at each side, in typical Romanesque style, the roof continues on a lower level. The lovely large circular spoked *rose window*, surrounded by allegories of Fortune, in the centre of the façade is by Master Brioloto (reports on this artist place his activity between 1189 and 1220). The tendency nowadays is to attribute to him not only the design of the window itself, but the

▼ *View of the side and the façade of San Zeno*

▲ *General view of the porch*

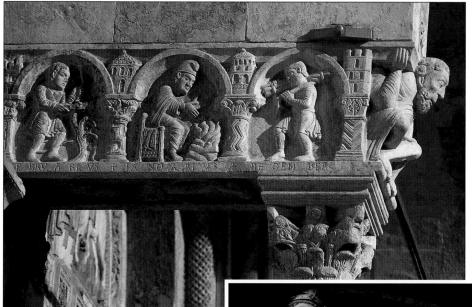

the earlier façade, to which it belonged. Above the doors stands a *Porch* supported by columns on standing lions, and the lintels are decorated with carvings in relief, showing representations of the *Months of the Year*, by an unknown artist. On each side of the arch: figures of *St. John the Baptist* and *St. John the Evangelist*. *St. Zeno, among Infantrymen and Knights of the City Council* is sculpted in bas-relief in the lunette above the door. The eighteen bas-relief panels on each side

▲ *Porch lintel decorated with carvings in relief depicting the Months (December, January, February)*

design of the whole complex façade. On the cornices of the sloping side roofs, a carved frieze by Adamino da San Giorgio (early 13th century).

The impressive *portal* of the church dates from about 1138, and is generally attributed to Maestro Nicolò. It was incorporated in the present façade after the demolition of

▲ *Detail of the lunette above the portal featuring St. Zeno and the Knights*

of the doorway also formed part of the earlier façade. They represent *scenes from the Old and the New Testament*, the *Duel between Theodoric and Odoacer*, and bottom right, *Theodoric Hunting Evil Spirits*. The latter is thought to be the work of Nicolò, while the others are attributed to his pupil Guglielmo. The doors are unique in that each one

◀ *Column-bearing lions on either side of the porch*

▲ ▼ *Bas-reliefs on the left side of the portal depicting the Nativity and the Adoration of the Magi*

▲ ▼ Bas-reliefs on the right side of the portal with the Original Sin and the Expulsion from Eden

▲ Bas-reliefs on the right side of the portal with the Creation of Adam, the Creation of Eve and the Creation of the Animals

◀ *Bas-relief with the Duel between Theodoric and Odoacer, on the left side of the portal*

INTERIOR. The interior of the church is a lovely combination of Romanesque and Gothic styles. The rigorous majesty of the structural elements stresses the historical importance of this basilica. The spacious interior is divided by cruciform piers and columns supporting sweeping arches. The central arch underlines the superb, tri-sectioned keel-shaped wooden ribbed Gothic ceiling. The church is built on three different levels: the *Lower Church*, occupying about two-thirds of the building, the *Upper Church* or raised Presbytery, and the *Crypt* beneath. The few steps leading down into the church are flanked by two *holy water stoups*. To the left: a *Baptismal Font* of monolithic design, attributed to Brioloto (12th century).

RIGHT AISLE. The walls and are covered with 13th and 14th century frescoes, of great importance in the history of Veronese art of this period.

bears 24 bronze panels depicting scenes from the *Old* and *New Testaments and the Miracles of Saint Zeno*. These panels are enclosed in borders of varied design with heads at each corner. In addition, the border of the right-hand door has the figures of *six Saints* and a *Sculptor*, while on the border of the left-hand door are 17 small panels depicting *Kings*, *Emperors*, and the *Virtues*. The bronze panels were transferred from the old doors when the entrance was enlarged during the early 13th century, and as a result, a few more had to be added around this time. Most of them, however, were cast in the early 12th century, and are attributed to a Veronese craftsman who came under the influence of Byzantine and markedly of Ottonian artists. Researchers are still trying to identify the author of the bronze

panels, but the extraordinarily vivid, "barbaric" energy of the figures, the originality and freedom of the imagery employed is a superb blend of tradition and seething renewal.

▶ *Bas-relief with Theodoric Hunting Evil Spirits, on the right side of the portal*

▲ *Portal bronze panels depicting the Descent into Hell, the Glory of Christ, the Beheading of St. John,*
the Expulsion from Eden, the First Labours and Fratricide, St. Zeno and the Messengers of Emperor Gallienus

▲ *Triptych with the Madonna and Saints, by Andrea Mantegna*

They depict, among others, *St. Christopher* (ca. 1300) and the *Madonna Enthroned*, by the "Second Master of San Zeno", a *Crucifixion* and *St. Stephen*, by the "First Master of San Zeno". Along the staircase and the wall of the raised Sanctuary are the *Madonna* by Martino da Verona, *St. George* by the "Second Master of San Zeno", and the *Baptism* and *Resurrection of Lazarus*, (13th century) and others. First altar on the right: *Madonna and Saints* by F. Torbido (16th century). Second altar on the right: built of marble taken from a 13th century porch.

◀ *Statue of St. Zeno, by an unknown 14th century artist*

PRESBYTERY. Statues of *Christ* and the *Apostles* by a local sculptor who was influenced by the Saxon school, stand along the top of the iconostasis or balustrade. At the top of the right wall is a votive fresco dating from 1397 (School of Altichiero). The *Sanctuary*, built by Giovanni and Nicolò da Ferrara in 1386-1398, is decorated with frescoes by Martino da Verona. On the high altar stands the *Triptych*, with *Madonna and Saints*, by Andrea Mantegna, painted between 1457 and 1459.

In the left apse stands an impressive statue of *Saint Zeno*. It is made of polychrome marble by an unknown sculptor of the early 14th century, and is much loved by the people of Verona. Next to the Sacristy door stands the *Statue of St. Proculus* by Giovanni da Verona (1392). On the wall is a *Crucifixion* which shows the influence of Altichiero, and two other versions of the *Crucifixion* by Turone and by the "Second Master of San Zeno". This wall also bears traces of many other frescoes.

▲ *View of the apse and the crypt*

CRYPT. A broad staircase leads down to the crypt. The arches are decorated with friezes in relief, by Adamino da San Giorgio dating to 1225 (probably the year when the crypt was completed). The arches and vaults of the crypt are supported by 49 columns, whose capitals are of great interest as each one is different. The central apse contains the urn holding the holy *body of Saint Zeno.* The crypt also contains several other sarcophagi, in particular those of *St. Lupicillius*, *St. Lucillius* and *St. Crescentian* (12th and 13th centuries).

LEFT AISLE. Baroque altar dedicated to *Our Lady of Sorrows.* At the end of the aisle, next to the entrance, stands the great monolithic *porphyry bowl*, probably of Roman origin. Legend, however, has it that the bowl was brought here by the devil. On the wall is the great *Crucifix* attributed to Guariento, and it is here that the *Carroccio* of the Commune of Verona was kept – when not in use – in the Middle Ages. The *Carroccio* was the war chariot on which the standard of the Free Commune of Verona was borne to the battlefield.

▼ *View of the ample Romanesque cloister, with the 13th century tower in the background*

▲ *The shrine in the cloister*

CLOISTERS. One enters the cloisters from the left aisle of the basilica. The effect is one of spaciousness, as the covered walks surround a large open grassy square. The arches on two of the opposing sides of the cloisters are Gothic, while those on the other two sides are rounded. Slim double columns support the arches. A charming, open shrine with piers and columns projects from one of the sides of the cloister, which also houses stone fragments and tombs. On the eastern side is the **Chapel of St. Benedict**, once probably a Roman hypogeum, or underground burial chamber, decorated with frescoes by the School of Giotto. The cloister offers a great view on the north side of the basilica and of the bell tower.

▶ *View of the apse of San Zeno*

CHURCH OF SAN BERNARDINO

It used to belong to the Franciscan Order. Founded in 1451, it was completed in 1466. It is preceded by a cloister. The façade is brick and has Gothic windows. *Statues of Franciscan Saints* stand above the lunette that crowns the main entrance (1474), whereas the lunette contains is decorated by a fresco depicting *St. Francis Receiving the Stigmata*.

INTERIOR. There is a single nave, a feature which is often found in Franciscan churches, as well as a side aisle and chapel on the right of the

▶ *The gallery in the cloister of San Bernardino*

church First chapel on the right: frescoes on the walls of *Episodes from the Life of St. John the Evangelist* by N. Giolfino, who also painted the *Episodes from the Life of St. Francis* on the

ceiling vault. Over the altar hangs a copy of the original painting by Cavazzola now in Castelvecchio. Second chapel on the right: *Madonna and Child with Saints*, by F. Bonsignori. Fourth chapel on the right: Frescoes by Dom. and Fr. Morone: The marble altarpiece depicts *Franciscan Saints*. Fifth chapel on the right: *Crucifixion*, a masterpiece by Fr. Morone dating from 1498. Also, *Mary and Jesus* by F. Caroto, the *Resurrection of Lazarus* by A. Badile, and the *Story of the Passion*, by N. Giolfino. The *Deposition from the Cross* is a copy of the Cavazzola original now in Castelvecchio.

◀ *Façade of the church of San Bernardino*

Behind an iron railing stands a group in polychrome stone, representing the *Lamentation over the Body of Christ*. **Cappella Pellegrini** (entrance to the right of the nave) built by Michele Sanmicheli around 1527 for Margherita Pellegrini. Sanmicheli used a centralized plan for his masterpiece. Lovely spatial proportions flow in classical stately harmony. There are two orders, with a coffered dome supported by a drum. The door and three altars open off the lower order. Niches and three-mullioned windows with columns succeed each other in the upper order. A *Madonna and Child with St. Anne* by B. India (1579) above the altar with *The Eternal Father and Sts. Joseph and Joachim* by Ottino (17th century) The *Sanctuary* frescoes by Michele da Verona were lost forever due to bombing.

LEFT WALL. The 1481 organ is beautifully decorated by Domenico Morone. The first altar is dedicated to the *Bresavola Family* and was designed by F. Bibiena in the 18th century. The altarpiece depicting *St. Peter of Alcantara* is by A. Balestra.

A door in the left-hand wall of the church leads to a graceful 15th century cloister. The lunettes in the cloisters are decorated with 15th and 16th centuries frescoes. The main cloisters give access to the ancient *Library* of the convent (today "Sala Morone"), decorated with frescoes in 1503 by Domenico and Francesco Morone. The painting on the end wall depicts the *Madonna Enthroned* surrounded by members of the Sagramoso Family; on the side walls: *Saints and Famous Members of the Franciscan Order*.

PORTA PALIO

This gateway takes its name from a *Palio* or horse-race which used to be run in the vicinity, mentioned by Dante in Canto 15 of the "Inferno". It was once known as the Porta di San Sisto and is Sanmicheli's masterpiece in his capacity as a military architect.

The outer façade is built of smooth square-hewn stones rigorously partitioned by paired columns, while the inner consists of five openings, in which classical simplicity merges with delightful Mannerist decoration. Behind the arches is a gallery. The gateway was built between 1542 and 1557.

▼ *The Porta Palio, a masterpiece by Sanmicheli*

CHURCH OF THE SANTISSIMA TRINITÀ

This is an example of Verona's Romanesque art. The church was founded around 1073, and consecrated in 1117. Only the northern apse remains of the earlier building: the porch, the other apses, and the bell tower were built around 1130.

The square bell tower, with its brick and thinly banded stone facing and the elegant, three-mullioned windows of the bell-chamber is supposed to have inspired the builders of San Zeno. The façade is Lombard in style, with a hanging porch and a porticoed atrium, where the *sarcophagus of Antonia da Sesso* (1421) can be seen.

▲ *The church of the Holy Trinity and its lofty bell tower with a brick facing*

▼ *The sarcophagus of Antonia da Sesso*

▲ *The interior of the church of the Holy Trinity*

JULIET'S TOMB AND FRESCOES MUSEUM

The final goal of the pilgrim in search of Shakespeare's Romeo and Juliet is Juliet's tomb in the picturesque former Capuchin monastery, Via del Pontiere. Only the *cloisters* and the Baroque *Chapel of St. Francis* remain. The empty sarcophagus lies in a dimly lit crypt, and only reached this resting place after many vicissitudes. A long, but disputed tradition has it that this is the tomb of Shakespeare's heroine.

▲ *The cloister of the church of San Francesco al Corso*

▼ *Juliet's tomb*

The nearby *G.B. Cavalcaselle Frescoes Museum* hosts a series of wall paintings detached from old Veronese buildings, while interesting works of art from the 16th to the 18th century are on display in the *church of San Francesco al Corso.*

▼ *St. Celsius,*
by an 12th century Veronese artist

▲ *The Annunciation, by Louis-Dorigny*

▼ *Adoration of the Magi, by Antonio Palma*

◀ *The Three Archangels,
by G.F. Caroto*

▲ *Lust,
by Torquato
della Torre*

▼ *The Holy Trinity, by Antonio Balestra*

▲ *Washing of the Feet, by Caroto*

CHURCH OF SAN FERMO MAGGIORE

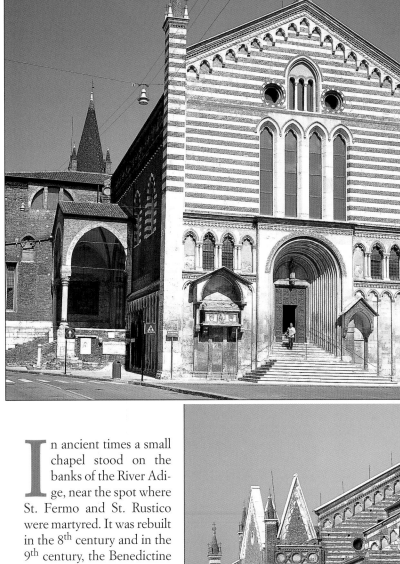

◀ *The Church
of San Fermo Maggiore*

▼ *View of the apse
of San Fermo Maggiore*

In ancient times a small chapel stood on the banks of the River Adige, near the spot where St. Fermo and St. Rustico were martyred. It was rebuilt in the 8th century and in the 9th century, the Benedictine Friars began work on a much larger structure in which, from the start, one of the two churches erected on the site, was intended to be built above the other. The lower church, the two lesser apses and the bell tower which was not completed until the 13th century all belong to the Benedictine project. The date of 1065 which appears in the lower church, probably refers to the year in which the

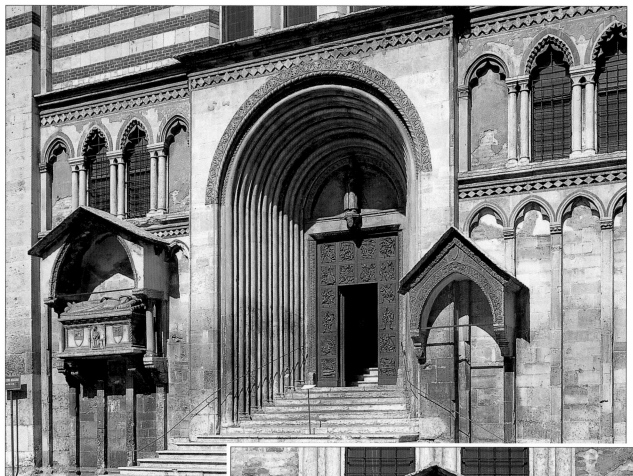

▲ *The splendid portal flanked
by the canopied tombs
of Aventino Fracastoro
and Giovanni da Tolentino*

Benedictine part was started, whereas
the building was restructured and
given its present appearance by the
Franciscans, who took over the complex after 1313. The great Gothic
upper nave and the splendid apsidal
complex were built above the pre-
existing Romanesque lower church.
The two styles merge into each other
harmoniously, thanks to the unity of
the colour scheme maintained throughout the complex. The apsidal sec-
tor of the upper church has delightful interwoven decorations and richly
ornamented arches.

► *The funerary monument
of Aventino Fracastoro*

FAÇADE. The varied openings in the façade progress, diminishing in scale, up to the point of the roof, from the great recessed Main Door, flanked by two canopied *Tombs* (left: *Monument to Aventino Fracastoro* – physician to the Scala family – who died in 1368; the frescoes which used to decorated the tomb are now in the museum of Castelvecchio). Right: the canopied *Tomb of Giovanni da Tolentino*) and by mullioned Gothic windows, to a great four-mullioned Gothic window topped by a smaller three-mullioned window and two round port windows, above which a series of pensile arches define the simple gable-shaped top of the façade.

The usual entrance to the church is on the left side where a staircase, covered by a massive porch, leads up to the door. 13th century frescoes in the lunette (the one on the left by Fr. Morone, 1523).

INTERIOR OF THE UPPER CHURCH. Of typical Franciscan design, with a single nave, it has a 14th century multi-keel-shaped wooden ribbed ceiling, decorated with images of *Saints*. The church is primarily famous for the quality and number of its 14th and 15th century frescoes. In the lunette above the main door is the *Crucifixion*, attributed to Turone. On the opposite wall are fragmentary 14th and 15th century frescoes, including a *Last Judgement* by Martino da Verona.

RIGHT WALL. 14th century fresco representing the *Martyrdom of Franciscan Friars*. Above the 16th century *Nichesola Altar* is a *Madonna and Saints* by S. Creara, while the lunette is by D. Brusasorci. The detached fresco, *Angels with a Scroll*, is by Stefano da Verona. The Pulpit (1360) was commissioned by a lawyer, Barnaba da Morano, and is surmounted by a Gothic canopy. The frescoes surrounding it are by Martino da

▼ *The interior of San Fermo Maggiore*

Verona. The *Annunciation* – a fresco – on the upper section of the wall, clearly reveals Giotto's influence. On the walls of the Brenzoni Chapel (15th century) are the *Tomb of Bernardo Brenzoni* (died 1494), and the *Funeral Monument of Barnaba da Morano*, decorated with statues and fine reliefs, probably by Venetian artists. The third altar, known as the *Saraina* (16th century), used to be in the Church of the Holy Trinity (Santissima Trinita). On the altar front is a 15th century *Deposition*. The fine altarpiece shows *The Holy Trinity, Madonna and Saints* and is by Fr. Torbido. The fifth altar was architecturally inspired by the Roman Gavi Arch.

RIGHT APSE. *Crucifixion*, by D. Brusasorci. Then comes the *Sanctuary*, highlight of the Basilica, in front of which there is a semi-circular screen (1523). Above the triumphal arch, frescoes (about 1314), which depict the kneeling figures of *Prior Daniele Gusmerio* and *Guglielmo di Castelbarco*, and which clearly reveal the influence of Giotto. There are other important 14th century frescoes on the wall: the *Coronation of the Virgin*, *Adoration of the Magi* and the *Stories of the Franciscan Friars*. Behind the 18th century sanctuary altar there are rare wooden choir stalls (15th century). The vault of the ceiling above the apse is decorated with 14th century frescoes, depicting the *Symbols of the Four Evangelists*. Above the altar in the nearby *Chapel of St. Anthony* hangs Liberale da Verona's outstanding *Saints Anthony, Nicholas and Augustine. Monument to the Della Torre Family*, in the rectangular chapel beside the left wall, a splendid example of the sculpture of A. Briosco, called Il Riccio, with richly carved marble sections and superb bas-reliefs in bronze. The originals of the bronze reliefs – now in the Louvre Museum, in Paris – are replaced by copies.

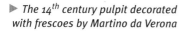
► *The 14th century pulpit decorated with frescoes by Martino da Verona*

▲ *The funerary monument
to Nicolò Brenzoni, by Nanni di Bartolo*

Above it, subtly harmonising with the architectural lines, are the figures of the *Almighty* and the *Archangels Raphael* and *Michael*. This fresco is a masterpiece of the artist's early period and is a work of great importance in the study of northern Italian Gothic art.

LOWER CHURCH. Built around 1065, this church is an outstanding and rare example of early Veronese Romanesque architecture. The great nave, separated from the aisles by piers, has double arches supported by a row of smaller piers. The varied shapes of the ancient capitals are noteworthy, together with the 13th and 14th century frescoes on the walls and piers.

▼ *The interior of the lower church
with a nave and two aisles*

LEFT WALL. The Baroque *Lady Chapel*, with a *Madonna and Saints*, a masterpiece by F. Caroto above the altar. A 1363 fresco of the *Crucifixion* above the side door. The 1535 *Chapel of the Helmsmen* (Cappella dei Nocchieri) contains *Saints Nicholas, Augustine and Anthony* by Battista del Moro, the *Monument to Nicolò Brenzoni* by the Florentine artist Nanni di Bartolo, who sculpted a *Resurrection* all around the urn between 1424 and 1426. In these years Pisanello painted one of his most famous frescoes on the surrounding wall – the outstanding *Annunciation*.

Porta dei Leoni

Yet another monument bequeathed by the Romans, dating from the middle of the 1st century B.C. It was once part of the ancient city walls, and was drastically altered about a hundred years after its construction. It consisted of two arches topped by a tympanum and flanked by columns, above which rose a series of arched windows, and finally a large exedra. The rear of the existing section is concealed

▲ *Excavated area in the Via dei Leoni, with remains of the Roman city walls and a tower, two metres below the street level*

by a building immediately behind it, but the visible part corresponds more or less to the centre of the original gate. This gate, which is one of the most precious mementos of Roman Verona, was much admired by the artists of the Renaissance period for its perfect proportions and the beauty of its ornamentation. Recent thorough archaeological digs, the results of which are clearly visible from the street, have revealed the base of the ancient Roman gateway, extensive sections of the original road surface and the polygonal base of one of the great corner towers, defending the gateway.

◄ *The Lion Gate dating back to Roman times*

PALAZZO POMPEI - MUNICIPAL MUSEUM OF NATURAL HISTORY

On the Lungadige Porta Vittoria we can see this outstanding palazzo formerly known as Palazzo Lavezola, built by Sanmicheli in the years of his maturity (1530 or 1550), when his reputation was firmly established. It is one of his great works, and shows a very strong classical influence, despite concessions to the style of the time and the purpose of the building. The impressive facade, divided into two storeys, and the well-proportioned internal courtyard are of particular interest.

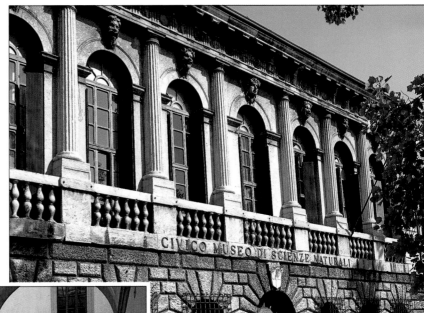

▲ Façade of the Palazzo Pompei, housing the Municipal Museum of Natural History

▲ The inner courtyard of the Museum

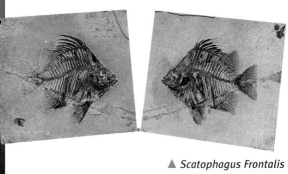

▲ Scatophagus Frontalis

This Palazzo has long housed the **Museum of Natural History**, which is famous throughout Italy and Europe.

There are over 20 rooms, containing rare collections, and the following fields are represented: mineralogy, palaeontology, biology, ornithology, icthyology, entomology, etc.

▶ The Room of Eocenic Fossils

▼ *Exposition of stratigraphic geology*

▲ *Showcase in the Room of Rocks*

◄ *Mineralised trunk*

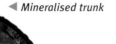

These are some of the more important rooms: **Room I** contains a very fine collection of *Eocene fossils* from the Bolca region. This includes a large number of animal and plant species which existed more than 30 million years ago. **Rooms II** and **III** are dedicated to collections of *minerals* and *stones*. **Rooms V, VI, VII,** and **VIII** are devoted to *mammals*. **Rooms IX, X, XI** and **XII** are devoted to all aspects of *ornithology*. **Rooms XIII** and **XIV** contain exhibitions of *fish*, *reptiles* and *amphibians*. The collection of *insects* in **Room XV** is of great interest. The remaining rooms deal with *invertebrates*, *palaeontology*, and *prehistory*, among other subjects.

▼ *Dombeyopsis*

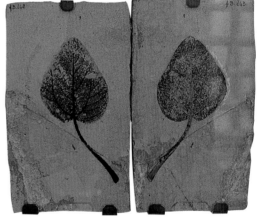

◄ ▼ *The Quaternary Room and a showcase in the Room of Mushrooms*

This church, built between 1464 and 1483, was once part of a Benedictine monastery. A large cloistered courtyard in front has an imposing entrance built in 1688. The façade is made of brick with an outstanding gothic portal and Renaissance windows. The bell tower was built around 1552.

The interior consist of a main nave flanked by two aisles with three apses.

RIGHT AISLE. The *Annunciation*, by P. Farinati (1557) hangs above the second altar. *Adam and Eve* in the lunette are by the same painter. *Ecce Homo*, by O. Flacco, above the fourth altar.

SACRISTY. The 15th century wall *cupboards* are decorated with marquetry. There is a 15th century triptych depicting the *Pietà* and *Saints Benedict and Francis*. The *Madonna and Saints* is by F. Brusasorci. The sections of a polyptych by Bartolomeo Montagna show *Saints Blaise and Juliana* and *Christ on the Sepulchre*.

SANCTUARY. Is decorated with impressive *frescoes* and four paintings depicting *Episodes from the Life of St. Celsus* by P. Farinati. There are another two pieces by Montagna, representing *Saints Benedict and John the Baptist*, and *Saints Nazarus and Celsus*.

The **Chapel of San Biagio**, in the left transept, was built by Beltramo di Valsolda in 1488, and consecrated in 1529. The plan is rectangular with a dome and a polygonal apse. Above the main arch is a painting of the *Annunciation* by P. Cavazzola (1510). There is a splendid marble altar with the *Sarcophagus of Saints Blaise and Juliana* by Bernardino Panteo (1508), altarpiece by Fr. Bonsignorio (the *Martyrdom of Two Saints*, and a *predella* by Girolamo dai Libri). Formerly, G.M. Falconetto and D. Morone decorated the vaults of the dome, while the great fresco on the walls, depicting stories of the life of Saint Blaise, is a masterpiece of Bartolomeo Montagna (1504-1505).

LEFT AISLE. The fifth chapel contains the *Madonna and Saints* by D. Brusasorci. In the third chapel there is the *Miracle of Saint Maurus* by G. Carpioni, and the *Madonna in Glory with Saints* by Antonio Badile is in the second chapel.

◀ *Entrance portal to the courtyard in front of the church*

▲ *Façade of the church of Santi Nazaro e Celso*

GIUSTI GARDENS

These gardens belong to the 16th century **Palazzo Giusti**. Entrance is from Via Giusti. They are amongst the finest late Renaissance gardens in the whole of Italy, and date from 1580. They are divided into two sections – the lower part being in the Italian style. The layout is spacious, with flower beds, a maze, statues, fountains etc., and a cypress avenue winding up the small hill topped by the Church of San Zeno in Monte, which was much admired by Goethe. There is a tower-shaped building with a winding staircase and a platform on top, from which one enjoys a magnificent view over the city.

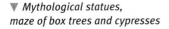
▼ *Mythological statues, maze of box trees and cypresses*

▲ *A fountain spout in the shape of a grotesque mask*

▲ *A scenic mascaron belvedere on the hilltop, originally designed to spit out tongues of flame from the mouth*

▲ *Italian-style trimmed box hedges and a mythological statue*

This church belonged to the monks of the Order of the Mount of Olives, and was redesigned in its present form in 1481. The lower part of the façade was built over an older original, and is attributed to Sanmicheli. The bell tower, however, with its domed top, was designed by Fra Giovanni da Verona.

INTERIOR. It is in Renaissance style with a nave, two aisles and a raised presbytery. The walls of the central nave are decorated with frescoes depicting *Stories from the Old Testament*, those on the right by Francesco Caroto, and those on the left by N. Giolfino.

RIGHT AISLE. *Madonna and Saints* by Antonio Balestra in the first chapel and the *Journey of St. Joseph* by G.B. Pittoni (18th century). *St. Michael* by P. Farinati in the second chapel.

PRESBYTERY. In the chapel opening off the end wall, on the right, flanked by frescoes by Cavazzola, *Santa Francesca Romana*, an altarpiece by Guercino (1639). The chapel to the right of the sanctuary contains frescoes by N. Giolfino, and Cavazzola's *Annunciation*. In the left chapel are *frescoes* by D. Brusasorci and *St. Benedict* by S. Bretagna. A work by Luca Giordano depicting the *Blessed Bernardo Tolomei* can be seen on the altar at the end of the left wall. The paintings in the sanctuary, by P. Farinati, depict the *Massacre of the Innocents* and *Stories from the lives of Saint Gregory and Saint Peter*. On the lower portion of the wall, a series of small *Landscapes* by D. Brusasorci.

▼ *The church of Santa Maria in Organo*

**The choir stalls
of Santa Maria in Organo**

LOWER CHURCH. The entrance to the sanctuary is from the upper church. This is a particularly interesting example of early Romanesque Veronese architecture. It has a nave and two aisles. An important 14th century marble polyptych depicting a *Madonna and Saints* is on the altar in the apse.

▼ *An example of the wooden inlays
in the choir stalls*

CHOIR AND SACRISTY. In this part of the church are the greatest works of Fra Giovanni da Verona – the superb multi-coloured *wooden marquetry choir stalls*, some of the finest of their kind in Italy. They were done in the late years of the 15th century and in the early 16th century and consist of two rows of *choir stalls* in the lovely **Choir**. Fra Giovanni was the architect of the **Sacristy** (1504) where he also decorated the cupboards. The beautiful *candelabrum* of carved wood and the *lectern* which stand in the Choir are also by Fra Giovanni.

The frescoes in the sacristy depicting *Popes* and *Benedictine Monks* are by Domenico and Francesco Morone. The *Landscapes* and the lower portions of the wall cupboards are by D. Brusasorci. The altarpiece depicting *Saints Anthony and Francis* is by Orbetto. In a room near the Sacristy is a 13th century wooden sculpture of *Christ Riding on an Ass.*

LEFT AISLE. Fourth chapel, *Madonna and Saints* by Savoldo. Third chapel, *Madonna and Saints Augustine and Zeno*, F. Morone, 1503.

CHURCH OF SAN GIOVANNI IN VALLE

This very ancient church was rebuilt after the earthquake of 1117, and was again badly damaged during the last war. It has a nave, two aisles and three apses, and is built entirely of stone. It was of fundamental importance in the development of Verona's Romanesque style, and many similar churches were built after it. The apses, of which the right apse is more ancient, are noteworthy

FAÇADE. Severe and simple, it has side windows and a central mullioned window. The 15th century portal is of marble, covered by a porch.

In the lunette is an important fresco by Stefano da Verona, depicting the *Madonna and Saints*. The bell tower is Romanesque, with an upper section added in the 18th century. The remains of the cloister, along the right hand side of the church, are Romanesque like the tombstones.

INTERIOR. The atmosphere is particularly fascinating, with a narrow central nave in striking contrast with the wider side-aisles from which it is divided by a series of

◀ ▲ *Façade of San Giovanni in Valle and relics of the ancient cloister*

piers and columns with Corinthian capitals. The ceiling is supported by wooden cross-beams. A 17th century staircase leads up to the raised presbytery.

The **Crypt** is reached from the presbytery and has a nave and two aisles as well. It contains many traces of the original church. There are two rare examples of Early Christian sculpture – both *Sarcophagi.* The first, of *Saints Judas and Thaddaeus*, bears fine sculpture on the sides, and a lid added in 1395. The second, probably of Roman origin, has fluted sides, and niches containing the figures of a husband and wife, with *Saints Peter and Paul* on the sides.

◀ *Watchtower of the Ponte Pietra*

Verona had two bridges in Roman times, and only this one, formerly known as *Pons Marmoreus*, has survived. Fragments of the other bridge, known as *Postumio*, can be seen on the river banks not far from the Church of Santa Anastasia. Ponte Pietra was built with five arches in pre-Augustan times. The arch next to the right hand bank was rebuilt in 1298, together with the tall watch tower, by Alberto della Scala. The contrast between the material used in the original bridge and its reconstruction, makes it very picturesque. A large portion of the four arches on the left, and some of the piers were destroyed at the end of World War II, in April 1945. Their reconstruction is worth mentioning due to the fact that most of the old stones were reclaimed from the river.

▼ *The Ponte Pietra and the Shrine of Our Lady of Lourdes on the hill of San Leonardo in the background*

▲ *The cavea of the Roman Theatre, where concerts and performances are staged*

partly recovered, is flanked by the impressive ruins of the wings Unfortunately, very little remains of the imposing façade which once faced the River Adige. Set against the green tufa hills, crowned by the ancient Monastery of St. Jerome, the theatre is very impressive. Above the last tier of seats to the left is a *loggia* with marble columns which once formed part of the theatre, though it seems unlikely that this was its original position.

An unusual feature is the wide, deep trench dug into the tufa behind the theatre to separate it from the mountain side.

▼ *Load-bearing arches at different levels of the cavea and decorative arches of the upper portion of the Theatre*

This Roman Theatre, overviewing the portion of banks of the River Adige called Regaste Redentore, was built in the second half of the 1st century B.C. Successive constructions caused the theatre to disappear. The excavations which brought it to light were commenced by the archaeologist Andrea Monga in the middle of the 19th century and were finished rather recently. The theatre contains semicircular tiers of seats, partly rebuilt. The *stage*, which has only been

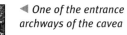

centuries, especially in the 17th century. A double Baroque staircase leads up to the church, with the door and a porch from the 14th century. Items of interest in the church include the following: an 18th century *Madonna and St. Gaetano* by Giambettino Cignaroli, in the first chapel on the left, the very fine *High Altar* decorated with inlaid marble panels and statues, the splendid *choir stalls* by three German artists: Kraft, Petendorf and Siut (1717-1720), and a painting of the *Annunciation* by Ridolfi. A *Bust of Pope Clement XIII* can be seen above the door.

Church of Santi Siro e Libera. Standing on the eastern side of the theatre, it is the only remaining building of the many which were built here over the years. It was founded in the 10th century and was remodelled over the

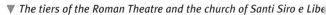

▼ *The tiers of the Roman Theatre and the church of Santi Siro e Libe*

▲ *View of the tiers of the Roman Theatre with the River Adige and the Ponte Pietra*

ARCHAEOLOGICAL MUSEUM

Access to this museum is by lift from the Roman Theatre. The museum occupies part of what was once the Monastery of St. Jerome. It offers the visitor a fund of information essential to an understanding of Verona in Roman times.

ROOM I (NEW ROOM).
Important mosaics among which *scenes of gladiatorial combat* dating from the 1st century A.D. The sculpture includes the *Head of a Prince of the Julio-Claudian Family*. and a *Bust of a Man in Armour*, both dating from the 1st century. The glass showcases contain a fine collection of pottery.

ROOMS II, III AND IV (MONKS' CELLS).
Sculpture, bronzes, glass etc. The bronzes include a *portrait of the Augustan era* and a *two-faced herm.*

▲ *Relics of mosaics with scenes of gladiator combats (I st cent. A.D.).*

▶ *Bust of a man in armour, of Roman period*

◀ *Relief depicting a scene of family life*

▲ *A room of the Archaeological Museum*

◀ *The Room of the Inscriptions*

▲ *Herm*

CORRIDOR. Roman sculpture, the most important of which is a statue of *Menander*. This is a Roman copy of the Julio-Claudian period, of a Greek original dating from the 3rd century B.C.

REFECTORY. Sculpture, urns from Volterra, inscribed gravestones, and mosaics. Among the sculptures is a *Seated Female Figure*, a Roman 2nd century copy of Venus-Aphrodite, whose Greek original dated back to the period of Phidias. Also of note are a *Statue of a Man*, which is a Roman copy of a 4th century B.C. Greek original, and a *Zeus Soter*, also copied from a Greek original.

Courtyard and Cloister of San Girolamo. Roman sarcophagi and tombstones from Verona.

Church of San Girolamo. An early Christian mosaic pavement is preserved here. The triumphal arch is decorated with a fresco by Caroto. *The Annunciation* (1508), and a 15th century *triptych* above the altar.

The second cloister was damaged in the 18th century. Fragments of sarcophagi are preserved here, together with a 2nd century *two-faced herm*, a *Head of Heracles* and others. Finally there is the **Nymphaion**, a part of the Roman building which probably once had some connection with the Theatre below. From here, visitors can have a lovely view of the city.

▶ *Cloister of San Girolamo with remains of stone slabs and mosaics*

CHURCH OF SANTO STEFANO

According to a tradition this church, a masterpiece of Verona's Romanesque architecture, was intended to be the city's first Cathedral. An oratory existed on the site as early as the 6th century, but it was destroyed by Theodoric and rebuilt in the 8th century. The present building, however, was founded in the 12th century and the apse is the result of 14th century alterations. The traditional stone and brick decoration on the façade, together with the stone pillars and the hanging porch above the entrance give the church a very fine appearance. An unusual aspect of the exterior is the robust octagonal *drum* above the crossing.

INTERIOR. Typical basilica design with a central nave divided from the aisles by powerful piers, and a raised presbytery section.

RIGHT AISLE. Noteworthy is the 14th century statue of *Saint Peter on a chair*. The *Chapel of the Innocents* (1619-1621) was frescoed by Ottino in Baroque style. The paintings depict the *Assumption* and the *Virtues*. The *Massacre of the Innocents* above the altar is also by Ottino. To the right is an important work by the most famous of all Veronese 17th century painters, Marcantonio Bassetti, showing the *Five Bishops of Verona*, to whom the chapel is dedicated. Facing it is the *Forty Martyrs* by Orbetto. In the lunette above the side door the fresco with *Saint Stephen and the Holy Innocents* is by Battista del Moro. The frescoes depicting the *Nursing Madonna* and *Christ and Mary Magdalene* date from late 14th century.

PRESBYTERY. This is the most important part of the church, and its outstanding feature is a rare *semicircular gallery*, the columns bearing capitals from the original 8th century church. There is also a *Bishop's Throne* of the same period which gave rise to the legend of this church's Cathedral status. The dome is decorated with frescoes by Domenico Brusasorci (1543); on the right side of the presbytery is a *Madonna and Saints Peter and Paul* by F. Caroto. The chapel to the left contains the frescoed *Annunciation* and the *Coronation of the Virgin*, attributed to the school of Stefano da Verona.

CRYPT. It is strikingly reminiscent of the deambulatory on the upper level. Several elements of the early building survive here, particularly the ancient *capitals* on the columns, and fragments of 13th century frescoes.

◄ ▲ *Façade and detail of the octagonal dome of Santo Stefano*

CHURCH OF SAN GIORGIO IN BRAIDA

This church was founded in 1447 and designed by Antonio Ricci. It was built on the site of a small 8th century church, dedicated to the same saint. Around the middle of the 16th century the drum and the cupola were designed by Sanmicheli. He was also responsible for the bell tower, which was never finished.

The facade is 17th century. French shot spattered the house next door in 1805. The damage is still visible.

INTERIOR. Not only is this church one of the richest in works of art in Verona, it is also outstanding for the quality of its design. It has one central nave, with side chapels opening off it. On the wall above the main door the *Baptism of Christ*, by Jacopo Tintoretto. At the beginning of the nave two remarkable 16th century *holy water stoups*, with statues of *St. John the Baptist* and *St. George.*

First chapel on the right: *Christ and Mary Magdalene* by F. Montemezzano (16th century). Second chapel on the right: *Assumption of the Virgin* by P. Ottino. Third chapel on the right: *Madonna and Archangels*, an outstanding work by Domenico Brusasorci. At either end of the choir stand two sections of a painting by Romanino depicting the *Judgement of Saint George* (16th century).

PRESBYTERY. On the balustrade are *statues of the Apostles* in bronze, similar in style to those on the holy water stoups. On one side is the *Annunciation Angel*, while the *Virgin* can be seen on the opposite side, They are both works by F. Caroto. The paintings at the sides of the high altar depict the *Multiplication of the Loaves* and *Manna falling from Heaven* by F. Brusasorci, completed by Ottino

and Turchi in the 17th century. Behind the altar hangs one of Paolo Veronese's finest works: the *Martyrdom of Saint George* (1565-1566). On each side of the 16th century organ is another work by Romanino in two sections, depicting the *Martyrdom of Saint George,* while paintings by Moretto da Brescia depicting *Saints Cecily, Agnes, Lucy and Catherine* (1540) can be seen on the altar below. In the fourth chapel on the left, one of the major works of Girolamo dai Libri, *Madonna and Saints Zeno and Lorenzo Giustiniani, with Angelic Musicians*. In the chapel on the left is a *Triptych* including the *The Transfiguration* by Francesco Caroto; the lunette is by Domenico Brusasorci. Second chapel on the left: *Martyrdom of Saint Laurence* by Sigismondo De Stefani (1564). First chapel on the left: *Saint Ursula and the Virgins* by F. Caroto.

▼ *The church of San Giorgio in Braida*

122

▲ *18th century façade of San Giorgio in Braida*

SHRINE OF OUR LADY OF LOURDES

The Shrine of Our Lady of Lourdes rises to dominate Verona from the hill of San Leonardo which encircles the Valdonega valley: the building sprang up in its present forms starting in 1958 owing to events that make it one of the most significant places in the contemporary ecclesiastical history of the whole city.

According to popular tradition, the Crusaders, on their return from the Holy Land, erected a series of oratories in the Valdonega area, because of the resemblance of its landscapes with places in Palestine. Thus, one church was dedicated to St. Mary of Nazareth, a second one to Saint Mary in Bethlehem, and a third one was called Holy Rood, in reference to the hill of Calvary at Jerusalem.

On the hill of San Leonardo, from at least 1265 there rose a church dedicated to the Saint that had an adjoining monastery, the complex of which was to grow enormously before the dreadful earthquake that struck Verona in 1511. Today, only the Romanesque bell tower, a part of the cloister and the apse of the church

▼ *The hill of San Leonardo and the Shrine of Our Lady of Lourdes*

▲ *The Shrine of Our Lady of Lourdes*

▼ *Statue of the Virgin, by Ugo Zannoni (1908)*

remain. In 1785, however, the monastery was de-consecrated until the hill was designated by Grand Duke Maximilian of Hapsburg as the seat of a military fortress due to its strategic position, that was realised in 1838. Finally, in the post-war years the complex, that had been used as a political prison between 1943 and 1945, was assigned to the Fathers of the Stigmata who erected a new shrine.

The Fathers had reached Verona shortly after the foundation of their order, in 1853. They had first settled in Piazza Cittadella, in what was called the Church of the Stigmata. Later, owing to an increase in the religious family, they moved to the church of St. Theresa which was reconsecrated to the Virgin of Lourdes, for which Ugo Zannoni sculpted a *statue of the Virgin* (1908) that was placed in

a special grotto. During the Allied bombing of Verona in 1945, the Church of the Stigmata was destroyed, but the statue of the Madonna remained miraculously undamaged. In search of a new seat, the monks were assigned the old fortress on the hill of San Leonardo. The building of the present shrine was begun in 1958 to the design of architect Paolo Rossi, over the structures of the ancient fort and with the adoption of a large body with a circular plan and protruding wings, realised with the most modern technologies involving the use of concrete. The *statue of the Virgin* was lodged in a modern new grotto on a terrace, so as to create in this way two places for worship: the actual church and the space outside the grotto open over the city.

1. Arena (Roman Amphitheatre Romano)
2. Scala Family Tombs
   Church of Santa Maria Antica
3. Juliet's House
4. Romeo's House
5. Juliet's Tomb
   Church of San Francesco al Corso
   Frescoes Museum "G.B. Cavalcaselle"
6. Castelvecchio
   Municipal Museum of Castelvecchio
7. Roman Theatre
   Church of Santi Siro e Libera
   Archaeological Museum
   Church and Cloister of San Girolamo
8. Cathedral (Duomo)
   Chapter Cloister and Library
9. Basilica of Sant'Anastasia
10. Basilica of San Zeno Maggiore
11. Church of Santi Nazaro e Celso
12. Church of the Santissima Trinità
13. Church of San Bernardino
14. Church of San Fermo Maggiore
15. Church of San Giorgio in Braida
16. Church of San Giovanni in Fonte
17. Church of San Giovanni in Valle
18. Church of San Lorenzo
19. Church of San Pietro Martire
20. Church of Santa Maria in Organo
21. Church of Sant'Eufemia
22. Church of Santo Stefano
23. Shrine of Our Lady of Lourdes
24. Arch of the Gavii
25. Porta Borsari
26. Lion Gate
27. Porta Nuova
28. Porta Palio

29. Ponte Pietra
30. Ponte Scaligero
31. Corso Cavour
    Palazzo Carnesali
    Palazzo Scannagatti-Gobetti
    Palazzo Bevilacqua
    Palazzo Carlotti
    Palazzo Portalupi
    Palazzo Muselli
    Palazzo Canossa
32. Corso Porta Nuova
33. Piazza Bra
    Palazzo della Gran Guardia
    Palazzo Barbieri
    Palazzo Guastaverza
34. Piazza delle Erbe
    Domus Mercatorum
    Palazzo Maffei
    Casa Mazzanti
    Gardello Tower
    Torre dei Lamberti
35. Piazza dei Signori
    Palazzo del Comune
    Courtyard of the Mercato Vecchio
    Palazzo del Capitano
    Palazzo degli Scaligeri
    Loggia del Consiglio
    Domus Nova
36. Bishop's Palace
37. Palazzo Forti (Former Palazzo Emilei)
    Modern Art Gallery "Achille Forti"
38. Palazzo Giusti
    Giusti Gardens
39. Palazzo Pompei (Former Palazzo Lavezola)
    Municipal Museum of Natural History
40. Museo Lapidario Maffeiano